Have a Ball!

Basketball is a great game—to play, to watch, to talk about. It's a thrill-a-minute from the first dunk to the final buzzer. It's your favorite team fighting to make the playoffs and win the gold ring in the NBA Finals.

It's a made-in-America sport that began with a peach basket more than 100 years ago and today is an international game played and followed by millions the world over.

The NBA Book of Fantastic Facts, Feats & Super Stats is a bottomless basket of information. From amazing stories and quick quizzes to player profiles . . . from incredible performances and unmatched records to odd lists and facts about Dream Teams I and II . . . the book is designed to be a slam dunk.

The NBA Book of Fantastic Facts, Feats & Super Stats

The NBA Book

of Fantastic Facts, Feats & Super Stats

Edited by Zander Hollander

Rainbow Bridge®
Troll Associates

Photo Credits:
Cover: Andrew D. Bernstein, NBA Photos
Muggsy Bogues/Greg Forwerck, NBA Photos
Michael Jordan/Andrew D. Bernstein, NBA Photos
Gary Payton/Scott Cunningham, NBA Photos
Latrell Sprewell, Shawn Bradley, and Chris Mullin/Sam Forecich, NBA Photos
Charles Barkley/Andrew Bernstein, NBA Photos
Shaquille O'Neal/Andrew Bernstein, NBA Photos
Kevin Johnson/Bill Baptist, NBA Photos
David Robinson and Karl Malone/Chris Covatta, NBA Photos

Contents

■ ■ ■

Scottie Pippen, David Robinson, Joe Dumars,
Reggie Miller, Patrick Ewing, Karl Malone, John
Stockton, Clyde Drexler, Mark Price, Mahmoud
Abdul-Rauf, Chris Webber, Dennis Rodman,
Dominique Wilkins, Mitch Richmond, Larry
Johnson, Kevin Johnson, Alonzo Mourning,
Brad Daugherty, Kenny Anderson, Jim
Jackson, Jamal Mashburn, Shawn Kemp, John
Starks, Ron Harper, Otis Thorpe, Gary Payton,
Glen Rice, Charles Oakley, Vernon Maxwell,
Latrell Sprewell, Chris Mullin, Steve Smith,
Danny Manning, Clifford Robinson, Christian
Laettner, Derrick Coleman, Anfernee
Hardaway, Tim Hardaway

Acknowledgments

▬   ▬   ▬

Doc Naismith, the inventor, first envisioned basketball as a game any number could play. As editor of *The NBA Book of Fantastic Facts, Feats & Super Stats,* I proceeded along the same lines, although all was not play. Many hands had a role in the challenging task of researching and writing the book.

I thank Eric Compton of *Newsday*, an all-court ace; writers Dave Kaplan and Mitch Lawrence of the *New York Daily News* and Fred Kerber of the *New York Post* for their contributions. Also Bob Rosen of Elias Sports Bureau, master statistician Lee Stowbridge, historian Leonard Koppett, movie maven Jeffrey Lyons; Chip Lovitt, Rosanna Hansen, Carol Anderson, and Eileen Turano of Troll Associates, Phyllis Hollander of Associated Features, Christopher Drelich, and the NBA's Frank Fochetta, Diane Naughton, Clare Martin, and the team public relations directors.

Countless sources were used, including eyewitnesses, interviews, newspapers, Associated Features books, the Basketball Hall of Fame, *The Official NBA Basketball Encyclopedia*, NBA Photos, and *Leonard Maltin's Movie Video Guide*, among others.

Zander Hollander

The Destiny of
Hakeem the Dream

Everywhere he went in Lagos, Nigeria, people stared at him and kids taunted him because of his size. He was only 15 years old, but had grown to a height of 6'9".

Hakeem Abdul Olajuwon was miserable.

Every day, the boys in his neighborhood kept ridiculing him until he couldn't take it any longer. "I would get into fights," Olajuwon recalled. "Sometimes I would be ashamed of being so tall. I would wish I was normal height so I could be friendly with everyone."

Born January 21, 1963, in Lagos, the third child in a middle-class family of five boys and one girl, Hakeem loved sports. Since soccer was king in Nigeria, he became a goalie on his high school team. He also excelled in team handball, which in Nigeria is played on a soccer-like field with players running up and down the field and firing the ball toward a goal.

Then he started fooling around with a basketball, although he knew virtually nothing about the sport.

Nobody knew it would be the beginning of The Dream.

Recognizing Hakeem's raw athletic talents, Richard Mills, the Nigerian national basketball coach, made him the team's center, even though Mills had to teach the gangly novice how to dunk a basketball.

Then when Olajuwon turned 17, his parents, who

ran a thriving cement business, encouraged him to go to college overseas. A United States State Department employee arranged for the 6'11", 190-pound teenager to visit several college campuses in the United States. When Olajuwon arrived in New York, it was cold. He wanted to go to a warmer place, so he jumped on the next plane to Houston and never left.

Olajuwon enrolled at the University of Houston as a business student in 1980. Because the "H" is silent in Hakeem, he was incorrectly given the name Akeem, but he was too polite to correct the mistake. He waited until 1991 to announce he preferred the real Arabic spelling of his name, Hakeem, which means "wise one."

When Olajuwon first joined the school's basketball team, little was expected of him. He was a foreigner and basketball was still foreign to him. In fact, coach Guy Lewis withheld him from competition his first year to teach him the fundamentals and to add muscle and weight to his thin frame. "He had no power move to the basket, he had no turnaround shot," Lewis said. "He could jump, but he didn't know when to jump or where to jump."

"We knew he'd get better," said college teammate Clyde Drexler, who would later become an NBA star in Portland, "because he couldn't get any worse."

Actually, the 7-foot, 255-pounder's improvement became scary. In his sophomore year in 1982-83, he centered a run-and-gun Cougars team that won 25 straight games. Because of their high-flying, above-the-rim style, the Houston Cougars were nicknamed "Phi Slamma Jamma" as Olajuwon rapidly became one of the most awesome shot-blockers in college history.

In leading Phi Slamma Jamma to the NCAA championship game, a 54-52 loss to North Carolina

State, Olajuwon was named the tournament's MVP. He took Houston to the NCAA championship game again the next season, but the Cougars lost to Patrick Ewing and Georgetown, 84-75.

Feeling he had learned enough to compete with the best in the world, Olajuwon decided to forego his final year of college eligibility and enter the NBA Draft. The Houston Rockets made him the first overall pick in the 1984 Draft from a talent pool that also included Michael Jordan, Charles Barkley, and John Stockton.

Teamed with 7'4" Ralph Sampson to form "The Twin Towers," Olajuwon helped transform Houston into a defensive force with his shot-blocking, intimidating presence. Olajuwon worked tirelessly in the off-season to improve his offense, taking 500 shots a day, and soon became the NBA's premier all-around center. He averaged 30 points against Kareem Abdul-Jabbar in the 1986 playoffs as the Rockets eliminated the defending-champion Lakers. "In terms of raw athletic ability," marveled the Lakers' Magic Johnson, "Hakeem is the best I've ever seen."

Hakeem the Dream became a nightmare for opponents. His spin moves and fallaways were impossible to defend. Always a terror defensively, Olajuwon became the first player in NBA history to block 200 or more shots for 10 straight seasons. And he annually leads the league's centers in steals.

Yet Olajuwon always felt a void. For one, his parents never got to see him play in person; he sent tapes of his games home to Nigeria. For another, he had never won a championship.

With Olajuwon as the anchor, the Rockets opened the 1993-94 season with an NBA record-tying 15-0 streak. Hakeem averaged a career-high 27.3 points per game and won league MVP honors. He was also named Defensive Player of the Year as the Rockets set a franchise record for fewest points allowed.

But the most rewarding part came in June. Olajuwon outplayed his fiercest rival, Ewing, and lifted the Rockets over the Knicks in a grueling 7-game final series for Houston's first-ever basketball championship. Olajuwon was named MVP of the Finals.

It seemed as if America finally discovered the true greatness of this proud athlete from Nigeria.

A devout believer in Islam, Olajuwon calls it "the overriding factor in my life." Yet he is grateful for his chance to play pro basketball, and appreciative that he has climbed to the top of his profession. "Looking back to see how far I have grown in my career and also how the NBA has grown, I'm thankful," he said.

Hakeem is a collector of abstract art and likes to relax by painting in oils. He lives on the outskirts of Houston, but now has a fan following across the world. Nowhere more than Lagos, Nigeria, where nobody is making fun of him anymore.

Year	Team	G	FG	FG Pct.	FT	FT Pct.	Reb.	Ast.	TP	Avg.
1984-85	Houston	82	677	.538	338	.613	974	111	1692	20.6
1985-86	Houston	68	625	.526	347	.645	781	137	1597	23.5
1986-87	Houston	75	677	.508	400	.702	858	220	1755	23.4
1987-88	Houston	79	712	.514	381	.695	959	163	1805	22.8
1988-89	Houston	82	790	.508	454	.696	1105	149	2034	24.8
1989-90	Houston	82	806	.501	382	.713	1149	234	1995	24.3
1990-91	Houston	56	487	.508	213	.769	770	131	1187	21.2
1991-92	Houston	70	591	.502	328	.766	845	157	1510	21.6
1992-93	Houston	82	848	.529	444	.779	1068	291	2140	26.1
1993-94	Houston	80	894	.528	388	.716	955	287	2184	27.3
Totals		756	7107	.516	3675	.705	9464	1880	17899	23.7
Playoff Totals		85	902	.531	492	.724	1045	259	2298	27.0

Shaq Magic in Disney World

For Shaquille O'Neal, it was a mismatch. He missed his old friends back in the United States, missed listening to rap music, missed being one of the fellas again. Living in a foreign country simply made him miserable.

The son of a strict U.S. Army sergeant, Shaquille lived on military bases in Germany from ages 12 to 15. He hated every minute of it and did everything he could to make his father send him back. He got into all sorts of trouble—fights and other teenage mischief. But his dad, Philip Livingston, was tough and did not hesitate to discipline his son.

Shaq finally got tired of arguing with his father. "I came to realize that it was better to get rewarded than punished," Shaq recalled.

For Shaq, who was born March 6, 1972, in Newark, New Jersey, basketball would be his reward. He was 6'7" by the time he was 14 and was so clumsy he couldn't even dunk. He had grown so fast and was hampered by Osgood-Schlatter's disease, which caused discomfort in his knees. But he kept practicing, kept improving, and kept out of trouble.

"My father is a strong man and he always tried to transfer that strength to me on the basketball court," Shaquille said. "Your ball, your court, your game. That's what he used to tell me. That was his credo."

One day, Shaq's father told him some wonderful news. He was being transferred back to the United States. The family would relocate in San Antonio, Texas. "I was an American again, and it felt great," Shaq said, "not to mention what it did for my basketball career."

At Robert Cole High School, which was on the army base in San Antonio, Shaq became a one-man army himself. He led his teams to a 68-1 record, prompting a flock of college coaches to personally recruit him, including Dean Smith of North Carolina. But Shaq settled on Louisiana State. He and his father always liked LSU coach Dale Brown, who held a basketball clinic in Germany when Shaq was 13.

The pressure and expectation for Shaquille, who had grown to 7-feet and 285 pounds, was enormous. One year, he was on the cover of nine preseason magazines. And the games weren't always fun, either. He frequently had three or four defenders hanging on him, he once suffered a broken leg, and he was provoked into a fight that got him thrown out of the Southeastern Conference Tournament in his junior year.

Although Shaq was the 1991 College Player of the Year and led LSU to three straight NCAA Tournament berths, he felt he'd had enough. So he became available for the 1992 NBA Draft and was selected No. 1 overall by the Orlando Magic.

Few could have predicted the impact the 20-year-old center would have on an entire league.

By then, 7'1" and 303 pounds, Shaq cut an awe-some figure on the court—never more so than when crashing the boards with his arena-rattling dunks. With his affable personality and exuberant smile, Shaq became an overnight sensation who created "Shaq Mania."

Packing in enthralled crowds wherever he played, he made the second-year Magic the second-best draw on the road, next to Michael Jordan and the Chicago Bulls. And in Orlando, the home of Disney World, he became a super attraction.

As Hall-of-Famer Bob Cousy said, "In the next five years, Shaquille O'Neal is going to be the most recognizable athlete in the world. He's going to dwarf Michael Jordan."

Actually, Shaquille might be ahead of schedule. Already almost as marketable as Jordan in his NBA heyday, Shaq's also as strong as Wilt Chamberlain, to whom he's often compared. In Shaq's rookie year, his trademark rim-rocking dunks broke the hydraulic basket supports. Such episodes have caused the league to create a "Shaq Rule," requiring a spare basket support. He became the youngest player ever to be selected for the All-Star Game and won Rookie-of-the-Year honors, averaging 24.1 points a game.

But the best way to measure O'Neal's on-court impact is to look at what he's done since he donned No. 32 in black, silver, and blue. Before he arrived in Orlando, the Magic was a 21-61 team. In O'Neal's first season, they won 41 games. His second season, 1993-94, they won a franchise-best 50 games and made the playoffs for the very first time.

"He has so much talent and so much potential still, it's very scary," Hall-of-Fame coach Chuck Daly said.

One weakness in Shaq's game is his foul-shooting. He is only a 57-percent shooter, but vows "it'll come" through concentration and practice.

Of course, much of his game is already in place. Shaq averaged 29.3 points a game in his second season (he lost the NBA scoring title when David

Robinson scored 71 points on the final day of the season). He was such a 1-man powerhouse, he pulled down 28 rebounds and blocked 15 shots in one game. And in the summer of 1994, he dominated the World Championships as the leader of USA Dream Team II.

With brilliant point guard Anfernee Hardaway, the O'Neal-Hardaway combination is projected to do for the Magic in the 1990s what Magic Johnson and Kareem Abdul-Jabbar did for the Lakers in the 1980s.

Amazingly, the marketing of Shaq has only just begun. Only 22, he's already a talented entertainer (he starred in the basketball film *Blue Chips*), cut two rap records, and has been a potent pitchman for soda and sneakers. Today, stores contain Shaq toys, Shaq clothes, Shaq trading and greeting cards, Shaq video games, not to mention Shaq T-shirts and jerseys. All of which, of course, can be wrapped in Shaq wrapping paper.

As the NBA's thunder-dunking man-child, Shaquille O'Neal is rewriting the book on endorsement power. Just wait until he wins a championship.

Year	Team	G	FG	FG Pct.	FT	FT Pct.	Reb.	Ast.	TP	Avg.
1992-93	Orlando	81	733	.562	427	.592	1122	152	1893	23.4
1993-94	Orlando	81	953	.599	471	.554	1072	195	2377	29.3
	Totals	162	1686	.582	898	.572	2194	347	4270	26.4
	Playoff Totals	3	23	.511	16	.471	40	7	62	20.7

"Sir Charles" Rules as King of the Court

Outrageous and preposterous! That was the best way to describe a chubby high school sophomore in Leeds, Alabama, named Charles Wade Barkley.

Young Charles used to brag to friends that he would someday play in the NBA, but that only earned him laughter. After all, the only thing Charles loved more than basketball was eating, and the 5'10", 220-pound teenager was too heavy and too slow in the beginning to even make the Leeds' basketball team.

To improve his chances as a junior, Barkley made solitary trips to the court down the street, where he shot and rebounded far into the night. Then he would practice jumping back and forth over a 4-foot fence in his yard, an exercise that would increase his stamina and develop his vertical leap.

An extraordinarily intense competitor, Barkley made the team as a junior. The following year, he grew up and out to 6'4" and 240 pounds and played center, while showing ball-handling skills few centers or forwards possessed.

Born February 20, 1963, in Leeds, Charles was raised by his mother, who cleaned houses, and his grandmother, a beautician. He was always blunt, always rambunctious, and always made people notice him.

And when he went to Auburn on a basketball

scholarship, everybody noticed his hefty weight. For a time, he tipped the scale at more than 300 pounds, causing him to be tagged such nicknames as "Boy Gorge," "The Round Mound of Rebound," and "The Leaning Tower of Pizza." Before one game against the University of Tennessee, opposing fans ordered a pizza for Barkley and had the delivery man hand it to him on the court as he warmed up. "That kind of thing inspired me," Barkley said later.

However, Barkley's weight galled Auburn coach Sonny Smith. So did his lackadaisical attitude during practices. Smith punished Barkley by making him run up and down the steps of the football stadium.

It all paid off as Barkley became the school's fourth all-time leading scorer while leading the Southeastern Conference in rebounding in his freshman, sophomore, and junior years. After his junior year in 1983-84, Barkley was invited to try out for the U.S. Olympic team. Again, there were problems with the coach, who in this case was disciplinarian Bob Knight.

Barkley reported at 284 pounds, which did not please Coach Knight. Though he made a strong impression at the tryout, Barkley was cut. Yet Barkley shrugged off the failure to make the team. He decided to forego his senior season at Auburn and turn professional.

With the fifth pick in the 1984 Draft, the Philadelphia 76ers selected Barkley. He played all 82 games his rookie year, averaging 14 points and 8.6 rebounds coming off the bench. But Barkley again clashed with the coach, Billy Cunningham, who pushed him to get more out of his awesome ability.

No one doubted Barkley's abilities or intensity. But Barkley soon raised eyebrows with his sudden new maturity. By his second year, the 6'5" forward had trimmed down to 260 pounds. Soon he was labeled with the more respectable nickname "Sir Charles," and in 1986-87, he became the shortest player in NBA history to win the rebounding title (averaging 14.6 per game).

"The thing about Charles is his determination," observed veteran NBA center Robert Parish. Others noted his quick reflexes, in which he is often the first player to leave the ground when he jumps for a rebound.

An explosive force with infectious energy, Barkley quickly blossomed as the NBA's biggest showman. No one understood the inherent fun in basketball better than this outgoing performer, who loves people and loves to entertain.

A joy to watch, incredibly quotable, and a pitchman in numerous TV commercials, Barkley often seemed like the game's greatest ambassador. But he found it difficult to walk away from off-court confrontations.

"People sometimes get mad at me because I tell the truth," he once said. "But anybody who knows me, I think, likes me. I'm a very spontaneous person. My momma told me a long time ago to let my emotions out, not to be repressed."

After eight seasons in Philadelphia, Barkley was traded to the Phoenix Suns before the 1992-93 season for Jeff Hornacek, Andrew Lang, and Tim Perry.

Before joining the Suns, Barkley was a key figure on the Dream Team that steamrolled through the 1992 Barcelona Olympics. Then he became an instant smash in Phoenix, averaging 25.6 points a game and being named MVP as he carried the Suns to the 1993 NBA Finals, where they finally succumbed to Michael Jordan and the Bulls.

However, ailing knees and a bulging disk in his back made Barkley contemplate retirement. The injuries limited his effectiveness in 1993-94, although he still could explode at key times, like his 56-point performance against Golden State in the playoffs.

Barkley's fierce desire to win and his sense of humor, in which he regularly pokes fun at refs, opposing players, and teammates, have made him one of the most colorful characters in sports.

Now Charles, whose autobiography is titled *Outrageous,* says he might run for governor of Alabama one day, and people are taking it seriously. Especially his high school friends back in Louisiana, who discovered early that "Sir Charles" knows no bounds.

Year	Team	G	FG	FG Pct.	FT	FT Pct.	Reb.	Ast.	TP	Avg.
1984-85	Philadelphia	82	427	.545	293	.733	703	155	1148	14.0
1985-86	Philadelphia	80	595	.572	396	.685	1026	312	1603	20.0
1986-87	Philadelphia	68	557	.594	429	.761	994	331	1564	23.0
1987-88	Philadelphia	80	753	.587	714	.751	951	254	2264	28.3
1988-89	Philadelphia	79	700	.579	602	.753	986	325	2037	25.8
1989-90	Philadelphia	79	706	.600	557	.749	909	307	1989	25.2
1990-91	Philadelphia	67	665	.570	475	.722	680	284	1849	27.6
1991-92	Philadelphia	75	622	.552	454	.695	830	308	1730	23.1
1992-93	Phoenix	76	716	.520	445	.765	928	385	1944	25.6
1993-94	Phoenix	65	518	.495	318	.704	727	296	1402	21.6
Totals		751	6259	.562	4683	.734	8734	2957	17530	23.3
Playoff Totals		85	753	.529	513	.707	1126	362	2058	24.2

Muggsy Bogues Proves You're Never Too Small!

He was a 5-year-old at his first summer camp in Maryland. He was barely able to climb onto a metal folding chair at a picnic. His feet weren't close to the ground and his eyes were barely level with the table.

Muggsy Bogues was the smallest kid around.

But he wanted to be out front, leading. Every morning he pleaded to be the one to hold the U.S. flag while the children recited the Pledge of Allegiance.

Leon Howard, who directed the Lafayette Court Recreation Center in Baltimore, witnessed Bogues playing organized basketball at age eight. "You could tell he was going to be a star," he said. "You saw the way he walked—like a peacock, head up with a little strut. He wasn't afraid of anybody."

Today, at 5'3", 144 pounds, the shortest player in NBA history, Muggsy Bogues is still not afraid of anybody. And he draws respect for his game more than for his stature.

Now in his seventh season with the Charlotte Hornets, the mighty mite defies the greatest of odds as he competes against players who for the most part are a foot or more taller.

How does he survive? He's fast, quick, strong and tenacious. He never seems to tire. "I'm always trying to get a steal. I'm always pressuring my opponent, trying to throw him off his rhythm," says 29-year-old Muggsy. "I play each possession like it's the last one of the game. It comes from not wanting to give up. I exert everything I have until exhaustion."

"His size has a lot to do with why he's so effective," says Hornets coach Allan Bristow. "His center of gravity is very, very low. No one can take the ball away from him. You can't see him. You can't find him. Sometimes it looks like he's in two places at once."

Muggsy doesn't lift weights and he eats junk food. The only explanation he gives for his muscular legs and conditioning is that he rode his bicycle "all over Baltimore" as a child.

His mother, Elaine Bogues, wanted a girl. She already had two sons and a daughter. But on January 9, 1965, in Baltimore, Maryland, she had another boy, whom she named Tyrone Curtis. "I wasn't disappointed," she says. "He was born healthy."

Ty, as she calls him, grew up to be a basketball star at Dunbar High School and at Wake Forest University before the Washington Bullets made him a first-round NBA Draft choice in 1987.

The first thing he did with his pro money was to move his mother out of the Lafayette public housing project in East Baltimore, buying her a 4-bedroom home in Ellicott, Maryland.

Times had not always been good. Life in the projects was hard. "It was right outside my door— drugs, shooting, people getting killed," he says.

Bogues spent countless hours at the Lafayette rec center, and along the way one of his buddies, Dwayne Woods, gave him the nickname "Muggsy." This was for the Bowery Boys movie character, and because he had a habit of mugging players defensively.

Muggsy's Dunbar High teams had an amazing 59-0

run in the early '80s and produced four NBA players—Bogues, Reggie Williams, David Wingate, and the late Reggie Lewis.

At Wake Forest he led the Atlantic Coast Conference in minutes played and assists his last three seasons. The university retired his jersey.

He was the starting point guard for the U.S. team that won the 1986 World Championships in Spain, where the fans nicknamed him *la chispa negra*, "the black spark."

When the Bullets left Muggsy unprotected in the 1988 expansion draft, he became a Hornet. He buzzed and darted to new heights in the 1993 playoffs when the Hornets, in their first playoff appearance, defeated the Celtics in the first round, and took on the Knicks in the second round.

His jump shot, steal, and two free throws in the final minute gave Charlotte a spectacular 110-106 victory over the Knicks in Game 3 before the New Yorkers won the series.

His strongest supporters are his teammates. "How many times do I have to tell y'all this?" Larry Johnson asks. "It all starts with Muggsy. He sets the tone for everything. He is the sparkplug."

When he's not on the road, Muggsy is a happy family man—with wife Kim, daughters Tyisha and Brittney, and son Tyrone Jr.

Year	Team	G	FG	FG Pct.	FT	FT Pct.	Reb.	Ast.	TP	Avg.
1987-88	Washington	79	166	.390	58	.784	136	404	393	5.0
1988-89	Charlotte	79	178	.426	66	.750	165	620	423	5.4
1989-90	Charlotte	81	326	.491	106	.791	207	867	763	9.4
1990-91	Charlotte	81	241	.460	86	.796	216	669	568	7.0
1991-92	Charlotte	82	317	.472	94	.783	235	743	730	8.9
1992-93	Charlotte	81	331	.453	140	.833	298	711	808	10.0
1993-94	Charlotte	77	354	.471	125	.806	313	780	835	10.8
	Totals	560	1913	.457	675	.797	1570	4794	4520	8.1
	Playoff Totals	10	39	.476	10	.714	36	72	88	8.8

The Incredible Flight of Air Jordan

He was idolized from Barcelona to Tokyo . . . from Walla Walla, Washington, to Waukegan, Illinois. Basketball had never seen a celebrity like him before. He was Babe Ruth in baggy shorts.

Michael Jeffrey Jordan was an aerial artist, contorting his body in midair to make improbable shot after improbable shot. To millions, he became known simply as "Air Jordan."

On the court and off, Jordan soared to uncharted levels.

It was impossible not to get a charge watching him perform during his nine electrifying seasons with the Chicago Bulls. With his tongue hanging out, Jordan single-handedly made the Bulls the hottest draw in the NBA. It was no coincidence that when this modest young man from Wilmington, North Carolina, joined the league in 1984, overall attendance in the league rose 47 percent.

His hang-time on drives toward the hoop and sensational dunks seemed humanly impossible. Once, when he scored 63 points against the Boston Celtics in a playoff game, Larry Bird wondered if he might be "God disguised as Michael Jordan."

He brought excitement to the game on every level. It was Jordan, then a 19-year-old freshman, who hit a 17-foot jumper with 17 seconds left to lift North Carolina to the 1982 NCAA championship. It was

Jordan who was the main man of the U.S. gold-medal teams in the 1984 and 1992 Olympic Games. And it was Jordan whose spectacular clutch play carried the Bulls to three straight NBA titles (1991-93).

Born February 17, 1963, in Brooklyn, New York, the son of Deloris and James Jordan grew up in North Carolina and, in his early years, gave little indication of his future greatness. In fact, as a sophomore he was cut from the Laney High School basketball team in Wilmington.

A growth spurt saw him go from 5'11" to 6'3" and his career started to soar. He sparked North Carolina to its first national crown in 25 years. After being selected third overall by Chicago in the 1984 NBA Draft (behind Akeem Olajuwon and Sam Bowie), he began to shatter countless statistical and marketing standards.

In his first season, he was named Rookie of the Year after averaging 28.2 points a game. In his third season, he averaged 37.1 points to win the first of seven straight NBA scoring titles. Jordan also scored like no other player in any sport in endorsements.

Besides his unbelievable on-court accomplishments, the Jordan phenomenon can also be credited to his sincerity, his boyish smile, and his humble manner. All this, plus his extensive charity work, made him one of the most appealing athletes ever.

In the summer of 1993, Jordan's perspective on life changed forever. His father, who was perhaps his closest friend, was found murdered in North Carolina. In October, before the start of the 1993-94 season, Jordan stunned the basketball world and touched the hearts of millions when he announced his retirement at age 30.

He had accomplished everything he wanted in basketball. There were no more mountains to climb.

Jordan had won three regular-season MVP awards, three NBA Finals MVP awards, Defensive Player of the Year distinction, and those three consecutive championships. He left the game with a 32.3 career scoring average, the best in NBA history.

So he decided to pursue another challenge—baseball, which he hadn't played since his junior year in high school. But the magic that Jordan possessed on the hardwood was missing on the diamond. Hoping for a shot at the major leagues as an outfielder, he spent the summer of 1994 with the Birmingham Barons, the AA affiliate of the Chicago White Sox. But he lacked the years of training and experience to be an instant success in baseball. Still, Jordan was a smash at the gate, his presence attracting record crowds throughout the Southern League.

Despite his difficulties on the baseball diamond, Jordan's legacy is secure. No one will ever forget his basketball brilliance. He had it all—acrobatic body control, three-point shooting, pinpoint passing, tenacious defensive skills, and tremendous desire. And he was always thrilling to watch.

Year	Team	G	FG	FG Pct.	FT	FT Pct.	Reb.	Ast.	TP	Avg.
1984-85	Chicago	82	837	.515	630	.845	534	481	2313	28.2
1985-86	Chicago	18	150	.457	105	.840	64	53	408	22.7
1986-87	Chicago	82	1098	.482	833	.857	430	377	3041	37.1
1987-88	Chicago	82	1069	.535	723	.841	449	485	2868	35.0
1988-89	Chicago	81	966	.538	674	.850	652	650	2633	32.5
1989-90	Chicago	82	1034	.526	593	.848	565	519	2753	33.6
1990-91	Chicago	82	990	.539	571	.851	492	453	2580	31.5
1991-92	Chicago	80	943	.519	491	.832	511	489	2404	30.1
1992-93	Chicago	78	992	.495	476	.837	522	428	2541	32.6
Totals		667	8079	.516	5096	.846	4219	3935	21541	32.3
Playoff Totals		111	1411	.501	942	.834	741	738	3850	34.7

NBA
Special-lists!
— — —

Fred Kerber follows basketball around the clock and around the land for the *New York Post*. In his spare time, he likes to make lists. Basketball lists. What follows are samples of Kerber running the court.

The Actors

They flop. They scream in pain. They never committed a foul in their lives. These are the men who act on the court—act as if they've never, ever done anything wrong while everybody else is the bad guy. And if you watch closely, you'll see them get away with lots. The envelope, please.

 1. Danny Ainge, Phoenix
 2. Reggie Miller, Indiana
 3. John Starks, New York
 4. Bill Laimbeer, Detroit (retired, but he was the best)
 5. Rick Mahorn, New Jersey
 6. Scottie Pippen, Chicago
 7. Christian Laettner, Minnesota
 8. J.R. Reid, San Antonio
 9. Kevin Johnson, Phoenix
10. Shaquille O'Neal, Orlando
11. Charles Barkley, Phoenix

The Air Up There

Ever wonder how those giant players keep from banging their heads when entering a doorway? Yeah, they've learned to duck. Here are the tallest players, according to their listed heights, who have made life miserable at one time or other for all those short guys in the NBA under 7-feet tall. Oh, and we stop this all-time list after seven players at 7'3" height because there are so many of those "ordinary" 7'2" guys.

1. Manute Bol, Washington, Philadelphia, Miami Golden State (7'7")
2. Gheorghe Muresan, Washington (7'7")
3. Shawn Bradley, Philadelphia (7'6")
4. Chuck Nevitt, Houston, L.A. Lakers, Detroit (7'5")
5. Mark Eaton, Utah (7'4")
6. Rik Smits, Indiana (7'4")
7. Randy Breuer, Milwaukee, Minnesota, Atlanta, Sacramento (7'3")

Passports, Please

These men were born elsewhere but came to America with more than their suitcases. Obviously, they came with a lot of basketball skills. And it didn't take them long to get accustomed to the American way on the basketball court.

1. Hakeem Olajuwon, Houston (Nigeria)
2. Patrick Ewing, New York (Jamaica)
3. Detlef Schrempt, Seattle (Germany)
4. Dikembe Mutombo, Denver (Zaire)
5. Dino Radja, Boston (Croatia)
6. Toni Kukoc, Chicago (Croatia)
7. Rik Smits, Indiana (Holland)
8. Rony Seikaly, Golden State (Lebanon)
9. Olden Polynice, Sacramento (Haiti)
10. Sarunas Marciulionis, Seattle (Russia)
11. Carl Herrera, Houston (Trinidad)
12. Gheorghe Muresan, Washington (Romania)
13. Vlade Divac, L.A. Lakers (Yugoslavia)

Davy Crockett Award

Davy Crockett was a famous frontiersman who could shoot the eyes out of a mosquito at 100 feet. Well, maybe he wasn't THAT good, but he could shoot from far away—just like these guys, the 10 men with the most 3-point field goals ever in the NBA. All except Larry Bird are still active.

1. Dale Ellis 1,013
2. Danny Ainge 924
3. Michael Adams 906
4. Reggie Miller 840
5. Terry Porter 729
6. Mark Price 699
7. Chuck Person 684
8. Derek Harper 681
9. Larry Bird 649
10. Vernon Maxwell 634

Fashion Parade

Want to know why some NBA types make SOOOO much money? It's so they can dress the way they do. Yes, when the game is over they like to slip out of their uniforms and into something comfortable—and usually expensive. And it's not just the players. Here are ten of basketball's best-dressed guys.

1. Gerald Wilkins, Cleveland
2. Pat Riley, New York (coach)
3. Kevin Willis, Miami
4. Hakeem Olajuwon, Houston
5. Chuck Daly, TBS (former coach)
6. Dominique Wilkins, Boston
7. Rudy Tomjanovich, Houston (coach)
8. Malik Sealy, L.A. Clippers
9. Magic Johnson, L.A. Lakers
10. Bob Hill, San Antonio (coach)

Family Matters

Wouldn't you hate it if your little brother or your twin brother followed you around everywhere? Or if you had to do the same job as your father so everyone compared you? Well, that's what some of these guys have to go through. Here is a listing of some NBA brother combinations (mostly current players) or other players whose dads also were in the pros. And there's a brother-sister combo, too.

1. Twins Horace (Orlando) and Harvey (Portland) Grant
2. Mark (Cleveland) and Brent (Washington) Price
3. Dominique (Boston) and Gerald (Cleveland) Wilkins
4. Jon (Milwaukee) and father Rick (Hall of Famer) Barry
5. Danny (Cleveland) and father Bob (former NBA player) Ferry
6. Dan (Lakers) and father Dolph (Hall of Famer) Schayes
7. Charles (Pistons) and Caldwell, Major, and Wil (ex-players) Jones
8. Rex (Washington) and father Ed (ex-ABAer) Chapman
9. Danny (Phoenix) and father Ed (ex-player) Manning
10. Chuck (San Antonio) and Wesley (Phoenix) Person
11. Reggie (Indiana) and Cheryl (USC and U.S. Olympic team) Miller

Did You Hear the One About . . .?

They may not have their own TV series, but NBA players are regular guys with funny, often bizarre, outlooks on things. Some are practical jokers. Back in Boston, Danny Ainge once wore a Herman Munster mask while at a dinner honoring teammate Kevin McHale. Some offer different insights (just listen to any of Charles Barkley's views on the world), and some are just downright funny (John Salley). Here is a sampling of the guys who have made the media laugh the most.

1. Charles Barkley, Phoenix
2. John Salley, Miami
3. Doc Rivers, New York
4. Tim Hardaway, Golden State
5. Danny Ainge, Phoenix
6. Mike Gminski, (retired)
7. Dwayne Schintzius, New Jersey
8. Charles Oakley, New York
9. Horace Grant, Orlando
10. Karl Malone, Utah

Real Names

You didn't really think anyone would name their children "Muggsy" or "Spud" or "Tree" did you? Well, here are the real first names of some famous players who are better known by their nicknames or, in some cases, their middle names.

1. TYRONE Muggsy Bogues
2. ANTHONY Spud Webb
3. WAYNE Tree Rollins
4. JACQUES Dominique Wilkins
5. BENJAMIN B.J. Armstrong
6. DARON OSHAY Mookie Blaylock
7. DeCOVEN Dee Brown
8. GLENN Doc Rivers
9. LAFAYETTE Fat Lever
10. CHARLES Buck Williams
11. JEROME Pooh Richardson
12. HERMAN J.R. Reid
13. ELLIOTT Dale Ellis
14. THEODORE Blue Edwards
15. VERNELL Bimbo Coles

The Brains

Not all games are won with muscle and leaping ability. Sometimes, you have to outthink and outwit your opponent. Here are some of the players who are regarded as among the smartest in the league.

1. Joe Dumars, Detroit
2. Craig Ehlo, Atlanta
3. Tim Hardaway, Golden State
4. Doc Rivers, New York
5. James Worthy, L.A. Lakers (retired)
6. Kevin Johnson, Phoenix
7. Mark Price, Cleveland
8. Scottie Pippen, Chicago
9. Mark Jackson, Indiana
10. John Stockton, Utah
11. Lee Mayberry, Milwaukee
12. Mookie Blaylock, Atlanta
13. Reggie Miller, Indiana
14. David Robinson, San Antonio
15. Danny Ainge, Phoenix
16. Nate McMillan, Seattle
17. Buck Williams, Portland
18. Chris Mullin, Golden State

The Selling Game

You see them on the basketball court, and then they pop up on the tube in a commercial or occasionally in a movie. Here are some of those super hoopsters whose popularity has brought them more fame and fortune.

1. Michael Jordan—Gatorade, McDonald's, Ballpark Franks, Nike, Hanes (No letup in sight despite his retirement from basketball.)
2. Shaquille O'Neal—Pepsi, Reebok, Hallmark
3. Larry Johnson—Converse ("Grandmama")
4. David Robinson—Nike (Mr. Robinson's "Neighborhood")
5. Patrick Ewing—McDonald's, Ewing Sportswear
6. Charles Barkley—Right Guard, Reebok
7. Dominique Wilkins—McDonald's, Minute Maid
8. Coach Pat Riley—Lincoln-Mercury
9. Karl Malone—L.A. Gear
10. Jamal Mashburn—Fila ("Mash, Crash, Smash")

Gallery of Stars

Some have made it big already and are called superstars. The others are well on the way. They're as young as Washington's 21-year-old Chris Webber and as ancient but still vital as "The Human Highlight Film," Boston's 34-year-old Dominique Wilkins.

It's one imposing cast of players whose profiles follow.

SCOTTIE PIPPEN
Amazing Bull

Scottie Pippen loves to get in his boat and cruise around Lake Michigan. "It lets me get away from it all," said the 6'7", 210-pound, Chicago Bulls' forward.

His opponents would prefer to see Pippen at sea rather than on court. His rise to NBA superstardom has been one of the game's stirring stories.

Pippen didn't even play high school basketball in Ham-burg, Arkansas, where he was born September 25, 1965. He attended Central Arkansas, a small school, and, as a freshman, showed little promise when he averaged only 4.3 points.

But by the time Pippen was a senior, NBA scouts were following his every game. He became an NAIA (National Association of Intercollegiate Athletics) All-American and the Seattle SuperSonics made him the fifth overall draft pick in 1987. But they traded him immediately to the Bulls for Olden Polynice and a No. 1 pick.

It wasn't long before the graceful Pippen established himself as a standout defensive performer, his quickness enabling him to guard smaller players and his long arms permitting him to repulse bigger opponents.

He has been on the NBA's All-Defensive First Team three times and, with his shooting and passing as well, played an enormous role alongside Michael Jordan when the Bulls won three championships in a row in 1991-92-93.

Pippen has played in four All-Star Games, until 1994 in the shadow of the magnificent Jordan. This time Pippen was the MVP. It was all part of another fine season marked by his leading the Bulls in scoring (22.0 for eighth in the NBA) assists and steals (second in the league).

What was next for Pippen? A leisurely cruise on Lake Michigan.

Year	Team	G	FG	FG Pct.	FT	FT Pct.	Reb.	Ast.	TP	Avg.
1987-88	Chicago	79	261	.463	99	.576	298	169	625	7.9
1988-89	Chicago	73	413	.476	201	.668	445	256	1048	14.4
1989-90	Chicago	82	562	.489	199	.675	547	444	1351	16.5
1990-91	Chicago	82	600	.520	240	.706	595	511	1461	17.8
1991-92	Chicago	82	687	.506	330	.760	630	572	1720	21.0
1992-93	Chicago	81	628	.473	232	.663	621	507	1510	18.6
1993-94	Chicago	72	627	.491	270	.660	629	403	1587	22.0
	Totals	551	3778	.491	1571	.683	3765	2862	9302	16.9
Playoff Totals		110	765	.472	426	.733	848	573	2016	18.3

DAVID ROBINSON
"The Admiral"

It was never boring, but it was always the same. For seven straight seasons, Michael Jordan was the NBA scoring champion. But in 1993-94, with Jordan taking his swings on the diamond, there would be a new champion.

Playing on the last day of the season, David Robinson of the San Antonio Spurs went on a 71-point spree against the Los Angeles Clippers. It was just enough to give him the new title with a 29.8 average (2,383 points) to runner-up Shaquille O'Neal of the Orlando Magic (29.3, 2,377).

For the man they call "The Admiral," it was a spectacular finish to another great season. The first center to lead the league in scoring since Buffalo's Bob McAdoo in 1975-76, the 7'1", 235-pound Robinson also contributed more assists (4.8) than any other center or forward in the NBA.

Robinson simply climbed another level in a storybook career. Born August 6, 1965, in Key West, Florida, he entered the Naval Academy after playing only one year of high school basketball (Osbourne Park, Manassas, Virginia). He was a 6'6", 175-pound freshman small forward at Annapolis with few basketball aspirations.

A standout student, he had a combined score of 1,320 (out of 1600) in the Scholastic Aptitude Test. When he was 14, he was taking advanced computer courses in a local college.

As a Navy freshman, he averaged only 7.6 points, but he soon sprouted in size, growing seven inches in two years. From then on he was unstoppable, becoming the College Player of the Year in 1987 and setting tons of records.

He was a member of the U.S. bronze-medal team at the 1988 Olympic Games in Seoul, Korea, after he was chosen No. 1 overall by the Spurs in the 1987 NBA Draft. But he had to fulfill two years of navy service before he took his first shot as a pro in 1989.

He's reaped awards galore since then: Rookie of the Year, twice All-NBA First Team, twice All-NBA Defensive First Team, among others. And he played on the gold-medal Dream Team in the 1992 Olympic Games at Barcelona, Spain.

Considering his many talents, he could have been a scientist or a musician. But never an admiral. That's because he grew too tall to remain in the service.

Year	Team	G	FG	FG Pct.	FT	FT Pct.	Reb.	Ast.	TP	Avg.
1989-90	San Antonio	82	690	.531	613	.732	983	164	1993	24.3
1990-91	San Antonio	82	754	.552	592	.762	1063	208	2101	25.6
1991-92	San Antonio	68	592	.551	393	.701	829	181	1578	23.2
1992-93	San Antonio	82	676	.501	561	.732	956	301	1916	23.4
1993-94	San Antonio	80	840	.507	693	.749	855	381	2383	29.8
	Totals	394	3552	.527	2852	.738	4686	1235	9971	25.3
Playoff Totals		28	233	.505	191	.705	340	85	657	23.5

JOE DUMARS
Dee-fense! Dee-fense!

Joe Dumars owns two NBA championship rings. And he didn't buy them at a sports collectors' convention. He earned them as a key player with the Detroit Pistons in 1989 and 1990.

A Piston from the beginning of a distinguished NBA career that began in 1985, the 6'3", 190-pound guard is a symbol of the ultimate team player. Four times he's made the NBA All-Defensive First Team and he has been an offensive force as well.

"Some guys take nights off in this league," said Chuck Daly, his former Detroit coach. "Not Joe. He plays all-out every game."

Born May 5, 1963, in Natchitoches, Louisiana, Dumars grew up in a football-focused family with five brothers and a sister. Brother David played in the United States Football League. But Dumars' game would be basketball. He was the all-time scoring leader at tiny McNeese State, and the Pistons chose him No. 18 in the 1985 Draft.

He made the All-NBA Rookie team in 1986 and was the MVP of the 1989 NBA Finals when he averaged 27.3 points per game. He has played in four All-Star Games.

Injuries hampered him in 1993-94, but he never gave up, and played for USA Dream Team II in the World Championship.

A favorite of the media because he is friendly and cooperative, Dumars gives to the community. In 1993, he began the "Joe Dumars Celebrity Tennis Classic," a charitable event that raises funds for Children's Hospital. He loves to play tennis when he's not caught up in the long season of pro basketball.

Year	Team	G	FG	FG Pct.	FT	FT Pct.	Reb.	Ast.	TP	Avg.
1985-86	Detroit	82	287	.481	190	.798	119	390	769	9.4
1986-87	Detroit	79	369	.493	184	.748	167	352	931	11.8
1987-88	Detroit	82	453	.472	251	.815	200	387	1161	14.2
1988-89	Detroit	69	456	.505	260	.850	172	390	1186	17.2
1989-90	Detroit	75	508	.480	297	.900	212	368	1335	17.8
1990-91	Detroit	80	622	.481	371	.890	187	443	1629	20.4
1991-92	Detroit	82	587	.448	412	.867	188	375	1635	19.9
1992-93	Detroit	77	677	.466	343	.864	148	308	1809	23.5
1993-94	Detroit	69	505	.452	276	.836	151	261	1410	20.4
Totals		695	4464	.473	2584	.848	1544	3274	11865	17.1
Playoff Totals		99	589	.466	381	.849	228	478	1591	16.1

REGGIE MILLER
Pulse of the Pacers

Reggie Miller of the Indians Pacers was struggling with his game, his shooting, and himself during the 1993-94 playoffs against the Knicks. That's when he talked to his sister Cheryl, a former All-American basketball player at Southern California and now the school's women's coach.

"She told me that I had to just be myself," said Reggie. "I had to be Reggie Miller."

The next game out, he was better than that. Spurred on by his sister's pep talk, the 6'7", 185-pound Miller put on one of the classic shooting displays in playoff history. His 25-point fourth quarter—third-highest in NBA annals—helped the Pacers defeat the Knicks in Game 5 of the Eastern Conference Finals. He hit five 3-pointers during his barrage, sending Madison Square Garden into a state of shock.

"That was Jordan-esque," said Knicks' coach Pat Riley. "What he did in that game was the closest someone has come to doing what Michael Jordan used to do."

But in the closing seconds of Game 7, with the Knicks leading by a point, he came up short on a jump shot that could have won it. And Miller and his teammates wound up watching the Finals on television.

Miller, who was born on August 24, 1965, in Riverside, California, could always shoot. Then again, he might be only the second-best shooter in his family. Yeah, he's got to deal with sister Cheryl, who, in addition to all else, was a member of the 1984 U.S. Olympic gold-medal team. She can still pop 'em, so maybe they should have a shootout to settle things once and for all.

As an All-American at UCLA, he was among the nation's top scorers as a junior and senior. He was selected with the 11th pick overall in the 1987 Draft by the Pacers. In his seventh season in the league, he finished third in 3-point accuracy. Adept at using picks and boasting a great release, he shot his way to No. 1 in all-time Pacer scoring. and he was a member of the USA Dream Team II.

"We had a great season," he said. "But I really wanted to make it to the NBA Finals.

Year	Team	G	FG	FG Pct.	FT	FT Pct.	Reb.	Ast.	TP	Avg.
1987-88	Indiana	82	306	.488	149	.801	190	132	822	10.0
1988-89	Indiana	74	398	.479	287	.844	292	227	1181	16.0
1989-90	Indiana	82	661	.514	544	.868	295	311	2016	24.6
1990-91	Indiana	82	596	.512	551	.918	281	331	1855	22.6
1991-92	Indiana	82	562	.501	442	.858	318	314	1695	20.7
1992-93	Indiana	82	571	.479	427	.880	258	262	1736	21.2
1993-94	Indiana	79	524	.503	403	.908	212	248	1574	19.9
Totals		563	3618	.498	2803	.877	1846	1825	10879	19.3
Playoff Totals		31	240	.487	205	.861	95	91	748	24.1

PATRICK EWING
Search for a Crown

The day Patrick Ewing rose to the top of the New York Knicks' all-time scoring list, he didn't want to talk about points. "I just want to win the championship," he said.

In 1993-94, co-captain Ewing's Knicks came as close as you can get. Playing in his first NBA Finals in nine NBA seasons, the 7-foot, 240-pound center had to endure the agony of defeat as the Houston Rockets edged the Knicks in seven games.

"It's no consolation that we went to a seventh game," said Ewing after his memorable showdown with the Rockets' Hakeem Olajuwon.

Ewing, born August 5, 1962, in Kingston, Jamaica, had always been used to winning. At Rindge & Latin High School in Cambridge, Massachusetts, he was the MVP in their state-championship season. And it was the same when he led Georgetown to three NCAA championship games, winning over Olajuwon and Houston in 1984.

He was the No. 1 pick by the Knicks in the 1985 Draft and Rookie of the Year in 1985-86 after playing for the U.S. gold-medal team in the 1984 Olympic Games. He would win another gold medal as a member of the Dream Team in the 1992 Olympic Games.

Considered the best jump-shooting center ever, with a deadly one-handed runner, Ewing has never averaged less than 20 points a season. And he has been dominant on defense. He set an all-time Finals record for blocked shots with 30 in the 1993-94 Finals. And he contributed 22 rebounds in the Eastern

Conference Game 7 that he won with a follow-up dunk against the Indiana Pacers.

"I really wanted to see the Knicks win so that Patrick could get the championship ring," said former Knick great Willis Reed. "Patrick has been a special player and nobody deserves it more than he."

Year	Team	G	FG	FG Pct.	FT	FT Pct.	Reb.	Ast.	TP	Avg.
1985-86	New York	50	386	.474	226	.739	451	102	998	20.0
1986-87	New York	63	530	.503	296	.713	555	104	1356	21.5
1987-88	New York	82	656	.555	341	.716	676	125	1653	20.2
1988-89	New York	80	727	.567	361	.746	740	188	1815	22.7
1989-90	New York	82	922	.551	502	.775	893	182	2347	28.6
1990-91	New York	81	845	.514	464	.745	905	244	2154	26.6
1991-92	New York	82	796	.522	377	.738	921	156	1970	24.0
1992-93	New York	81	779	.503	400	.719	980	151	1959	24.2
1993-94	New York	79	745	.496	445	.765	885	179	1939	24.5
Totals		680	6386	.522	3412	.742	7006	1431	16191	23.8
Playoff Totals		78	714	.474	365	.749	866	195	1799	23.1

KARL MALONE
"The Mailman"

As a player at Louisiana Tech, Karl Malone got the nickname "The Mailman"—because he always delivered.

When he's not pouring in points for the Utah Jazz, the 6'9", 256-pound forward hauls food, equipment, and all else in the off-season in his customized 16-wheel truck.

In traffic on the court or on the road, he's virtually unstoppable inside the lane. He uses his tremendous strength and also the feeds of teammate John Stockton.

"Karl is so big and strong, once he gets the ball inside you can put two points in the book," said Jazz coach Jerry Sloan. "The great thing is how hard he's worked and how far he's come."

Malone was born July 24, 1963, in Summerfield, Louisiana, and became Louisiana Tech's leading scorer and rebounder.

He was an early entry candidate in the 1985 NBA Draft, the Jazz taking him with the 13th pick. Malone was named to the All-Rookie team, has been All-NBA First Team five times, was MVP at the 1989 All-Star Game and co-MVP with Stockton at the 1993 All-Star Game.

He's No. 1 in franchise history in points and rebounds, and third in assists. Malone's 25.2 points per game in 1993-94 were his lowest average in seven years. His high was 31.0 in 1989-90, when he was topped by Michael Jordan's 33.6.

Despite playing a physical, pounding game, Malone has missed only four games in his 9-year career. He played on the Dream Team in the 1992 Olympic Games at Barcelona, Spain. He considers the Olympic experience one of his highlights—along with jumping in his truck and hitting the road.

Year	Team	G	FG	FG Pct.	FT	FT Pct.	Reb.	Ast.	TP	Avg.
1985-86	Utah	81	504	.496	195	.481	718	236	1203	14.9
1986-87	Utah	82	728	.512	323	.598	855	158	1779	21.7
1987-88	Utah	82	858	.520	552	.700	986	199	2268	27.7
1988-89	Utah	80	809	.519	703	.766	853	219	2326	29.1
1989-90	Utah	82	914	.562	696	.762	911	226	2540	31.0
1990-91	Utah	82	847	.527	684	.770	967	270	2382	29.0
1991-92	Utah	81	798	.526	673	.778	909	241	2272	28.0
1992-93	Utah	82	797	.552	619	.740	919	308	2217	27.0
1993-94	Utah	82	772	.497	511	.694	940	328	2063	25.2
Totals		734	7027	.525	4956	.719	8058	2185	19050	26.0
Playoff Totals		74	722	.477	573	.764	859	177	2018	27.3

JOHN STOCKTON
To the Rescue

Need an assist? The Utah Jazz know that John Stockton is always there with a helping hand. When Magic Johnson retired with the all-time NBA assist record (9,921), he said, "I know John Stockton is going to beat it. You can count on that."

Going into the 1994-95 season, Stockton (9,383) seemed a sure bet to add 539 assists and fulfill Johnson's prediction. In the previous seven years, except for 1992-93, the 6'1", 175-pound guard has never recorded less than 1,000 assists in a season.

"I get a lot of pleasure out of getting the ball to my teammates," Stockton said. "If I can make a good pass and help us win, it's as good as scoring a basket."

Born March 26, 1962, in Spokane, Washington, Stockton made his mark at Gonzaga University, where his grandfather had been an All-American halfback in the 1920s. A good student, Stockton made the Academic All-American second team as a senior.

The Jazz drafted him 16th for his smarts and skills in 1984. Since then he's set all sorts of assist records and has frequently drawn All-NBA Second-Team and All-Defensive Second-Team designations. But in assists, he's always No. 1.

Stockton has played in six All-Star Games, was co-MVP with teammate Karl Malone in the 1993 All-Star Game, and played with Malone as a member of the Dream Team in the 1992 Olympic Games at Barcelona, Spain.

Amazingly, he has missed only four games in 10 seasons.

Year	Team	G	FG	FG Pct.	FT	FT Pct.	Reb.	Ast.	TP	Avg.
1984-85	Utah	82	157	.471	142	.736	105	415	458	5.6
1985-86	Utah	82	228	.489	172	.839	179	610	630	7.7
1986-87	Utah	82	231	.499	179	.782	151	670	648	7.9
1987-88	Utah	82	454	.574	272	.840	237	1128	1204	14.7
1988-89	Utah	82	497	.538	390	.863	248	1118	1400	17.1
1989-90	Utah	78	472	.514	354	.819	206	1134	1345	17.2
1990-91	Utah	82	496	.507	363	.836	237	1164	1413	17.2
1991-92	Utah	82	453	.482	308	.842	270	1126	1297	15.8
1992-93	Utah	82	437	.486	293	.798	237	987	1239	15.1
1993-94	Utah	82	458	.528	272	.805	258	1031	1236	15.1
Totals		816	3883	.512	2745	.822	2128	9383	10870	13.3
Playoff Totals		84	421	.475	322	.821	269	929	1215	14.5

CLYDE DREXLER
"Clyde the Glide"

The 1989 Blazer Slam-Dunk Classic was down to its last player, Clyde Drexler. With the basket set at 11'1"—a full 13 inches above the standard NBA level—the 6'7", 222-pound guard began his approach, took off, and slammed the ball home.

It was only another winning dunk for Drexler, who has been one of the most exciting players in the NBA in the course of an 11-year Portland career. "Clyde the Glide" has few rivals who can match him in running the floor and scoring on fast-break opportunities.

Drexler has been hampered by various injuries in his last two seasons, but a strong finish in 1993-94 enabled him to contribute 19.2 points per game and sustain his steady rebounding.

He was born June 22, 1962, in New Orleans, Louisiana, and combined with Hakeem Olajuwon to lead the University of Houston to two straight trips to the NCAA Final Four. He was the first Houston player to score 1,000 points, snag 900 rebounds, and earn 300 assists in a career.

The Trail Blazers made him the 14th pick overall in the 1983 NBA Draft and over the years he's played in eight All-Star Games and has led Portland to two NBA Finals. He was chosen for the 1992 All-NBA First Team, and played on the Dream Team in the 1992 Olympic Games at Barcelona, Spain.

Drexler first drew attention for his dunks as a 6'6" senior in high school. "I've always liked to dunk," he said. "Hey, it's the easiest way to score. Right?"

Year	Team	G	FG	FG Pct.	FT	FT Pct.	Reb.	Ast.	TP	Avg.
1983-84	Portland	82	252	.451	123	.728	235	153	628	7.7
1984-85	Portland	80	573	.494	223	.759	476	441	1377	17.2
1985-86	Portland	75	542	.475	293	.769	421	600	1389	18.5
1986-87	Portland	82	707	.502	357	.760	518	566	1782	21.7
1987-88	Portland	81	849	.506	476	.811	533	467	2185	27.0
1988-89	Portland	78	829	.496	438	.799	615	450	2123	27.2
1989-90	Portland	73	670	.494	333	.774	507	432	1703	23.3
1990-91	Portland	82	645	.482	416	.794	546	493	1767	21.5
1991-92	Portland	76	694	.470	401	.794	500	512	1903	25.0
1992-93	Portland	49	350	.429	245	.839	309	278	976	19.9
1993-94	Portland	68	473	.428	286	.777	445	333	1303	19.2
Totals		826	6584	.480	3591	.786	5105	4725	17136	20.7
Playoff Totals		94	746	.450	464	.792	670	640	2015	21.4

MARK PRICE
The Price Is Right

The scene was John MacLeod's basketball camp at the University of Oklahoma in 1974. A 10-year-old boy stole the show.

The boy happened to be the son of MacLeod's assistant coach, Denny Price. His name: Mark.

"Back then, Mark could do it all," said MacLeod, who coached three NBA teams and now is at Notre Dame. "He could shoot, dribble between his legs and behind his back. He could run an offense. He was a natural."

Born February 15, 1964, in Bartlesville, Oklahoma, Price attended Georgia Tech, where he became the school's No. 2 all-time scorer. Many of the pro scouts felt that the 6-foot, 178-pounder was too short and too much of a shooter to play point guard in the NBA.

On draft day in 1986, the Dallas Mavericks selected Price with the 25th pick overall. But they never had any intention of keeping him. They traded him to Cleveland for a future pick and cash.

Price made the Mavs regret their mistake. He's been supreme as a point guard. As a shooter, he's .485 lifetime (.409 from 3-point range for fourth-best all-time in the NBA). His assists in 1993-1994 were ninth-best in the league. Deadly from the free-throw line, Price holds the NBA career record for free-throw percentage (.906).

"The thing that makes Mark so tough is that he's got one of the fastest releases in the game," said Phil Jackson, the Chicago Bulls' coach. "He's lightning quick."

Price made the All-NBA First Team in 1992-93, he's been selected to the All-NBA Third Team three times, and in 1994 he played for the USA Dream Team II.

Not only does Price's father still coach, at Phillips University, but his brother, Brent, is a guard for the Washington Bullets.

Indeed, the Prices have basketball in their blood.

Year	Team	G	FG	FG Pct.	FT	FT Pct.	Reb.	Ast.	TP	Avg.
1986-87	Cleveland	67	173	.408	95	.833	117	202	464	6.9
1987-88	Cleveland	80	493	.506	221	.877	180	480	1279	16.0
1988-89	Cleveland	75	529	.526	263	.901	226	631	1414	18.9
1989-90	Cleveland	73	489	.459	300	.888	251	666	1430	19.6
1990-91	Cleveland	16	97	.497	59	.952	45	166	271	16.9
1991-92	Cleveland	72	438	.488	270	.947	173	535	1247	17.3
1992-93	Cleveland	75	477	.484	289	.948	201	602	1365	18.2
1993-94	Cleveland	76	480	.478	238	.888	228	589	1316	17.3
Totals		534	3176	.485	1735	.906	1421	3871	8786	16.5
Playoff Totals		43	268	.476	170	.939	112	301	758	17.6

MAHMOUD ABDUL-RAUF
Crack Shot on the Foul Line

From how he looks, to how he plays, to what he calls himself, Mahmoud Abdul-Rauf of the Denver Rockets is a totally different player from the one who came out of Louisiana State in 1990.

Back then, the 6'1" Abdul-Rauf was known as Chris Jackson, star of the team, and he was selected third overall by the Denver Nuggets in the 1990 NBA Draft.

But after starting only 30 games in his first two seasons and not fulfilling expectations, the Nugget guard underwent big changes. He slimmed down his weight and regained the quickness that had made him an All-American sensation.

"The advice I received before I came into the league was I should get bigger," said Mahmoud-Rauf, who had ballooned to more than 190 pounds. "I had been told that I needed to be bigger to succeed in the NBA."

That turned out to be bad advice. In 1992-93, he improved his scoring from 10.3 to 19.2 points per game and was voted the league's Most Improved Player.

Much lighter at 160 pounds in 1993-94, he helped the Nuggets stun the basketball world when they became the first eighth-place seed in NBA history to defeat the No. 1 seed, the Seattle SuperSonics, in the opening round of the 1994 playoffs. The Nuggets went on to extend Utah to a seventh game in the Western Conference semifinals.

One area of Abdul-Rauf's game that didn't change was his free-throw accuracy. In 1993-94 he made 95.6 percent of his shots from the line—the second-highest percentage in NBA history—and he led the Nuggets in scoring for the second straight year.

Converting to the Islam religion, Jackson had changed his name before the 1993-94 season, becoming Mahmoud Abdul-Rauf. One thing hasn't changed for him, though. He still has to take medication for Tourette's Syndrome, a neurological disorder that results in uncontrolled tics and vocal utterances.

Despite his ailment, the Gulfport, Mississippi, native (born March 9, 1969) never lets it get him down.

"I never lost faith in my ability to play," he said. "My faith teaches me to strive for perfection."

He's closer to that than ever before.

Year	Team	G	FG	FG Pct.	FT	FT Pct.	Reb.	Ast.	TP	Avg.
1990-91	Denver	67	417	.413	84	.857	121	206	942	14.1
1991-92	Denver	81	356	.421	94	.870	114	192	837	10.3
1992-93	Denver	81	633	.450	217	.935	225	344	1553	19.2
1993-94	Denver	80	588	.460	219	.956	168	362	1437	18.0
	Totals	309	1994	.439	614	.921	628	1104	4769	15.4
	Playoff Totals	12	57	.370	29	.935	18	30	155	12.9

CHRIS WEBBER
Please, No Time-outs

Chris Webber will forever be remembered for one of basketball's greatest bloopers. During the final seconds of the 1993 NCAA championship game against North Carolina, he called a time-out when his Michigan team didn't have any left. The Wolverines drew a technical foul and lost their chance to beat North Carolina.

But Webber quickly recovered from that and also from the appendectomy that caused him to miss most of the Golden State Warriors' training camp in 1993. As the No. 1 overall draft pick, the 6'10" forward-center went on to become the first rookie in NBA history to total at least 1,000 points, 500 rebounds, 250 assists, 150 blocks, and 75 steals. The 250-pound Webber, who was the youngest player in the NBA in 1993-94, finished fourth in the league in shooting and ninth in blocked shots. As an impact, all-around player, Webber fulfilled everything the Warriors expected of him. However, in November 1994, in a surprise move, Webber was traded to the Washington Bullets for Tom Gugliotta and three future draft picks.

Born March 1, 1973, in Detroit, Michigan, Webber was chosen as 1990-91 National Player of the Year when he starred at Country Day High School.

An All-American at Michigan, he was a key to the Wolverines' back-to-back appearances in the NCAA Finals. He was the first sophomore to be selected with the No. 1 pick in the NBA Draft since Magic Johnson in 1979. Orlando drafted him and then he was traded to Golden State for No. 3, Anfernee Hardaway, and three future first-round picks.

When he arrived in the NBA, he said: "I feel like the luckiest man in the world. I just hope Muggsy Bogues [5'3"] guards me and maybe I'll score some points."

Year	Team	G	FG	FG Pct.	FT	FT Pct.	Reb.	Ast.	TP	Avg.
1993-94	Golden State	76	572	.552	189	.532	694	272	1333	17.5
Playoff Totals		3	22	.550	3	.300	26	27	47	15.7

DENNIS RODMAN
A Battler All the Way

He's no pussycat on or off the court. He's really a tiger. He has been suspended and fined for going too hard against his opponents. At times he has refused to practice or talk to the media. But nobody can disagree with former Detroit and New Jersey coach Chuck Daly when he says, "Dennis is one of the greatest defensive players I've ever seen."

In 1993-94, Rodman led the league in rebounding, averaging 17.3 boards per game. The No. 2 rebounder, Orlando's Shaquille O'Neal, averaged more than 4 fewer rebounds per game than Rodman.

It was in 1993-94 that Rodman brought his all-out hustle to San Antonio when he was traded with Isaiah Morris for Sean Elliott and David Wood. He had played for the Pistons in his previous seasons, figuring in a major role under the glass, and at the defensive end when the Pistons won back-to-back titles in 1989 and 1990.

Anyone who plays with Rodman marvels at how hard he plays, each and every game. His approach is simple. Every game is the seventh game of the NBA Finals.

"That's just me," he says. "That's my style. I don't know any other way to play."

He came out of tiny Southeastern Oklahoma State. At 6'8", he could jump with the best collegians and he had boundless drive. But the NBA teams passed on the 210-pound forward until Detroit took him with the 27th pick (second round) in the 1986 Draft.

Born May 13, 1961, in Trenton, New Jersey, he grew up in Dallas. But he never played high school basketball. Because of that, he wasn't recruited by the college basketball powers. He played at Cooke County Junior College in Texas before moving on to Southeastern Oklahoma.

The Pistons—and the rest of the NBA—quickly became aware of his aggressive skills and colorful personality. Twice he had been voted the league's top defensive player. And he has been a 5-time selection to the All Defensive First Team.

"Dennis taught me more about how to win—how to play winning basketball—than any other player I've ever played with," said his superstar teammate Dave Robinson. "His spirit and hustle are amazing."

Year	Team	G	FG	FG Pct.	FT	FT Pct.	Reb.	Ast.	TP	Avg.
1986-87	Detroit	77	213	.545	74	.587	332	56	500	6.5
1987-88	Detroit	82	398	.561	152	.535	715	110	953	11.6
1988-89	Detroit	82	316	.595	97	.626	772 *	99	735	9.0
1989-90	Detroit	82	288	.581	142	.654	792	72	719	8.8
1990-91	Detroit	82	276	.493	111	.631	1026	85	669	8.2
1991-92	Detroit	82	342	.539	84	.600	1530	191	800	9.8
1992-93	Detroit	62	183	.427	87	.534	1132	102	468	7.5
1993-94	San Antonio	79	156	.534	53	.520	1367	184	370	4.7
	Totals	628	2172	.537	800	.587	7666	899	5214	8.3
	Playoff Totals	97	271	.524	97	.500	814	82	641	6.6

DOMINIQUE WILKINS
"The Human Highlight Film"

Now playing in Boston, "The Human Highlight Film" is the perfect nickname for the acrobatic Dominique Wilkins, who has spun and dunked his way to NBA stardom.

No. 9 on the all-time NBA scoring list with 24,019 points, 'Nique averaged 26 points per game in 1993-94 with the Atlanta Hawks and Los Angeles Clippers. Traded by the Hawks in mid-season for Danny Manning, the 6'8", 218-pound forward became a Celtic in the summer of 1994 when he signed as an unrestricted free agent.

Born January 12, 1960, in Paris, France, where his dad served in the U.S. Air Force, Wilkins grew tall as a schoolboy sensation in Washington, North Carolina. His idol was the high-flying and future Hall-of-Famer Julius Erving.

When he left the University of Georgia to turn pro after his junior year in 1982, he was the school's leading scorer. Utah made Wilkins the third overall pick in the 1982 Draft, but he never played for the Jazz. In one of basketball's most lopsided deals, Utah traded him to the Hawks for John Drew, Freeman Williams, and cash.

Wilkins was a unanimous choice for the All-Rookie team in 1982-83, the only season in his 12-year career that he hasn't averaged more than 20 points.

His strong, gravity-defying moves propelled him to the All-NBA First Team in 1986 and he's been on the All-NBA Second Team four times. It is a rare year when he isn't an All-Star Game selection. Twice he has won the Slam-Dunk competition at All-Star Weekend.

Wilkins holds the fifth-highest scoring average in NBA history (26.5), has twice scored 57 points in a game, and holds the NBA record for most consecutive foul shots made in a game (23).

He's not the only member of his family to make it in the NBA. A younger brother, Gerald, has created his own highlights as one of the stars of the Cleveland Cavaliers.

Year	Team	G	FG	FG Pct.	FT	FT Pct.	Reb.	Ast.	TP	Avg.
1982-83	Atlanta	82	601	.493	230	.682	478	129	1434	17.5
1983-84	Atlanta	81	684	.479	382	.770	582	126	1750	21.6
1984-85	Atlanta	81	853	.451	486	.806	557	200	2217	27.4
1985-86	Atlanta	78	888	.468	577	.818	618	206	2366	30.3
1986-87	Atlanta	79	828	.463	607	.818	494	261	2294	29.0
1987-88	Atlanta	78	909	.464	541	.826	502	224	2397	30.7
1988-89	Atlanta	80	814	.464	442	.844	553	211	2099	26.2
1989-90	Atlanta	80	810	.484	459	.807	521	200	2138	26.7
1990-91	Atlanta	81	770	.470	476	.829	732	265	2101	25.9
1991-92	Atlanta	42	424	.464	294	.835	295	158	1179	28.1
1992-93	Atlanta	71	741	.468	519	.828	482	227	2121	29.9
1993-94	Atlanta	74	698	.440	442	.847	481	169	1923	26.0
Totals		907	9020	.467	5455	.813	6295	2376	24019	26.5
Playoff Totals		51	488	.429	350	.822	332	135	1345	26.4

MITCH RICHMOND
A High-Scoring King

You couldn't have found a happier player in the 1994 All-Star Game at Minneapolis than Mitch Richmond. A year before, the Sacramento Kings' 6'5", 215-pound shooting guard had to pull out of his first All-Star Game because of a hand injury. "That's what made making the All-Star team again so special," he said.

It was even more special because Richmond was voted to the West's starting five by the fans. He became the first player in Sacramento history to receive a starting berth.

"If anyone deserves it, it's Mitch," said Garry St. Jean, the Kings' coach. St. Jean should know. He was an assistant coach to Don Nelson at Golden State when the Warriors made Richmond their top pick in 1988 and the fifth player taken in the draft. But after three years with the Warriors, Richmond was traded to Sacramento for the rights to Billy Owens, the Kings' top draftee.

Despite going from playoff team to a team that has yet to make the post-season, Richmond has never let up. The player his teammates call "Rock" has raised his game.

"One of the best shooters around," said Seattle coach George Karl. "And he's got all that strength to get inside and score."

A crack shooter from outside (No. 7 in 3-point shooting and No. 7 in scoring in the NBA in 1993-94), he was Rookie of the Year in 1988-89 and made the All-NBA Second Team in 1993-94.

Born June 20, 1965, in Fort Lauderdale, Florida, Richmond is a powerful athlete who starred in football as well as basketball at Boyd High School. He played on the same high school team as the Dallas Cowboys' Michael Irvin. While Irvin was setting pass-catching records, Richmond was covering receivers as a defensive back.

He enjoyed a banner career at Kansas State and won a bronze medal as a member of the U.S. basketball team at the 1988 Olympic Games.

He credits his mom, Ernell O'Neal, with playing a

vital role in his career. "If not for her, I wouldn't be where I am today," he said. "She made me realize I had to be a better student to get anywhere."

Year	Team	G	FG	FG Pct.	FT	FT Pct.	Reb.	Ast.	TP	Avg.
1988-89	Golden State	79	649	.468	410	.810	468	334	1741	22.0
1989-90	Golden State	78	640	.497	406	.866	360	223	1720	22.1
1990-91	Golden State	77	703	.494	394	.847	452	238	1840	23.9
1991-92	Sacramento	80	685	.468	330	.813	319	411	1803	22.5
1992-93	Sacramento	45	371	.474	197	.845	154	221	987	21.9
1993-94	Sacramento	78	635	.445	426	.834	286	313	1823	23.4
Totals		437	3683	.474	2163	.835	2039	1740	9914	22.7

LARRY JOHNSON
Boxer Turned Hoopster

"In this corner . . . Larry Johnson . . . heavyweight cham-pion of the world."

Well, it might have happened. From the time he was 9 until he was 13, already more than 6-feet tall, Johnson loved to box in the Police Athletic League. He was considered a good prospect, but then he discovered basketball and became a playground legend in Dallas.

Today he's a 6'7", 250-pound monster forward with the Charlotte Hornets.

Born March 14, 1969, in Tyler, Texas, Johnson starred at Skyline High School in Dallas and, as a senior, was voted "most likely to succeed" by his classmates.

Indeed, he did succeed—first at Nevada-Las Vegas, where he gained All-American and Player-of-the-Year awards. He twice led the Runnin' Rebels to the NCAA Final Four, including one championship.

The Hornets made him the No. 1 overall pick in the 1991 Draft and he was Rookie of the Year. In 1992-93, he led Charlotte in scoring and rebounding, and became the first Hornet ever to appear in the All-Star Game. And he made the All-NBA Second Team.

He didn't miss a game in his first two seasons, providing muscle under the boards, the wing span of a jet plane, and one of the softest shooting touches in the game.

Johnson suffered from lower-back problems in 1993-94, causing him to miss 31 games, but that didn't keep him from playing with USA Dream Team II.

He's also known to the nation's basketball fans as "Grandmama" in a shoe-ad advertising campaign and has hosted his own charity game, "A Starry, Starry Night," in Charlotte.

Year	Team	G	FG	FG Pct.	FT	FT Pct.	Reb.	Ast.	TP	Avg.
1991-92	Charlotte	82	616	.490	339	.829	899	292	1576	19.2
1992-93	Charlotte	82	728	.526	336	.767	864	353	1810	22.1
1993-94	Charlotte	51	346	.515	137	.695	448	184	834	16.4
Totals		215	1690	.510	812	.778	2211	829	4220	19.6
Playoff Totals		9	68	.557	41	.788	62	30	178	19.8

KEVIN JOHNSON
Shining Brightly as a Sun

Michael Jordan reached the top of the mountain in basketball and then took on the challenge of baseball. In a way, Kevin Johnson—KJ—did the reverse.

The Phoenix Suns' point guard had been an outstanding shortstop in high school in Sacramento, California, before starring in basketball at the University of California. He so impressed the Oakland A's, they selected him in the 1986 baseball draft. Johnson played all of two games in the minor leagues, failing to get a hit and making one error in four chances.

Next stop: NBA.

He was born March 4, 1966, in Sacramento and was likened to a greyhound for his speed when he enrolled at California. The 6'1", 190-pound point guard made All-Pac 10 as a junior and senior, and the Cleveland Cavaliers took him at No. 7 in the 1987 NBA Draft.

In his rookie season, the Cavs traded him to Phoenix with Mark West and Tyrone Corbin for Larry Nance and Mike Sanders. It was one of the best deals the Suns ever made. From there on, he's been a smash hit, a Top-10 NBA finisher in assists, a productive scorer, and has played in three All-Star Games.

"In terms of breaking down the defense and getting to the basket, he's one of the best," said Utah coach Jerry Sloan.

Three times he's made the All-NBA Second Team and he's the Suns' all-time assist leader. His NBA single-game scoring high is 44 points, made against Utah in 1991-92. Johnson played for the USA Dream Team II at the 1994 World Championship.

He's not likely to try baseball again when his basketball days are over.

Year	Team	G	FG	FG Pct.	FT	FT Pct.	Reb.	Ast.	TP	Avg.
1987-88	Clev.-Phoe	80	275	.461	177	.839	191	437	732	9.2
1988-89	Phoenix	81	570	.505	508	.882	340	991	1650	20.4
1989-90	Phoenix	74	578	.499	501	.838	270	846	1665	22.5
1990-91	Phoenix	77	591	.516	519	.843	271	781	1710	22.2
1991-92	Phoenix	78	539	.479	448	.807	292	836	1536	19.7
1992-93	Phoenix	49	282	.499	226	.819	104	384	791	16.1
1993-94	Phoenix	67	477	.487	380	.819	167	637	1340	20.0
	Totals	506	3312	.494	2759	.837	1635	4912	9424	18.6
Playoff Totals		73	531	.470	467	.832	247	727	1541	21.1

ALONZO MOURNING
The World of "Zo"

"If you have a great defensive player, he makes everyone else better," said Allan Bristow, coach of the Charlotte Hornets. "Magic Johnson was a great offensive player and he made the other players better. 'Zo' has the same effect on defense."

"Zo"—otherwise known as Alonzo Mourning—has in two years become one of the premier centers in the game. Despite missing 21 games due to injuries in the 1993-94 season, he ended the year leading the Hornets in scoring, rebounding, and blocks (No. 4 in the NBA). A torn muscle in his left calf kept the 6'10", 240-pounder from playing in his first All-Star Game. But he was fit as a member of USA Dream Team II.

In his first season, Mourning was runner-up for Rookie of the Year to Orlando's Shaquille O'Neal, made the All-Rookie First Team, and became the Hornets' all-time shot-blocker in his 49th game. He finished the season with 271 blocks.

"The thing about 'Zo' is that he not only blocks shots but keeps them in play so we can have a chance to pick them up," said his teammate Larry Johnson. "We can't run if we don't stop somebody. But if we get the running going, it all breaks loose."

He is one of 49 foster children raised by Fanny Threet in Chesapeake, Virginia, where he was born February 8, 1970. He towered over all at Indiana River High School and landed at Georgetown University. There he made the Associated Press All-American team as a senior. Mourning was only the second player in Georgetown history to score more than 2,000 points and more than 1,000 rebounds. The other player? Patrick Ewing.

The Hornets drafted him second overall in 1992. Who do you think was first? Shaq O'Neal.

Mourning, whose college degree is in sociology, hasn't forgotten where he comes from. He's active with youngsters in depressed Charlotte neighborhoods and he serves as spokesman for a home for battered children. In these roles he's a far cry from the tough, explosive performer who puts the buzz in the Hornets.

Year	Team	G	FG	FG Pct.	FT	FT Pct.	Reb.	Ast.	TP	Avg.
1992-93	Charlotte..............	78	572	.511	495	.781	805	76	1639	21.0
1993-94	Charlotte..............	60	427	.505	433	.762	610	86	1287	21.5
	Totals	138	999	.509	928	.772	1415	162	2926	21.2
	Playoff Totals........................	9	71	.480	72	.774	89	13	214	23.8

BRAD DAUGHERTY
Centering the Cavs

Talk about growth spurts! In one year, Brad Daugherty grew an amazing 7 inches, which made him a 6'10" freshman when he entered high school.

That was the end of his growth period. He is still 6'10" and somewhat heavier at 263 pounds as the great passing center of the Cleveland Cavaliers.

Daugherty was born October 19, 1965, in Black Mountain, North Carolina. He entered the University of North Carolina as a 16-year-old freshman and was a starter after 10 games. He began his senior year by sinking 13 straight shots against UCLA.

He was a powerful rebounder and a prime candidate for the NBA. So prime that the Cavs made a deal to get him as the first pick in the 1986 Draft. Daugherty has teamed ever since with another 1986 rookie, Mark Price, the 25th selection.

In his first season, Daugherty was All-Rookie and he has built an impressive record thereafter. He has led NBA centers in assists for 6 of his 8 seasons and, no slouch as a scorer, he hit an astounding 57 percent of his shots in 1991-92 and 1992-93. Only injuries have kept him from being even better.

Daugherty is all-everything to the Cavs as their all-time point-maker and rebounder.

A true lover of nature, he says he'd be a fishing guide in Australia or Alaska if he hadn't found a home on the hardwood court.

Year	Team	G	FG	FG Pct.	FT	FT Pct.	Reb.	Ast.	TP	Avg.
1986-87	Cleveland	80	487	.538	279	.696	647	304	1253	15.7
1987-88	Cleveland	79	551	.510	378	.716	665	333	1480	18.7
1988-89	Cleveland	78	544	.538	386	.737	718	285	1475	18.9
1989-90	Cleveland	41	244	.479	202	.704	373	130	690	16.8
1990-91	Cleveland	76	605	.524	435	.751	830	253	1645	21.6
1991-92	Cleveland	73	576	.570	414	.777	760	262	1566	21.5
1992-93	Cleveland	71	520	.571	391	.795	726	312	1432	20.2
1993-94	Cleveland	50	296	.488	256	.785	508	149	848	17.0
	Totals	548	3823	.532	2741	.747	5227	2028	10389	19.0
Playoff Totals		41	275	.519	232	.756	419	137	782	19.1

KENNY ANDERSON
Toughest Net of All

Hall-of-Famer Jerry West always led the NBA in broken noses. Kenny Anderson hopes he doesn't follow suit in the broken-wrist department.

On February 28, 1993, the New Jersey Nets' point guard suffered a broken left wrist when he collided with the New York Knicks' John Starks. Anderson was out for the season and underwent surgery in the summer.

In 1993-94, he played from December until the Nets' final playoff game against the Knicks—almost 70 games—with another break in the same wrist.

"That's how tough Kenny is," said Chuck Daly, the former Nets' coach. "The wrist was hurting most of the season and he could have sat out the last month. But if he had, we wouldn't have made the playoffs."

After the season, his surgeon inserted a pin in the wrist and put it in a cast. Clearly, toughness and Anderson go together like popcorn and movies. He's a gutsy 6'1", 170-pounder who was born October 9, 1970, in Queens, New York, and drew national attention playing for Archbishop Molloy High School.

After two years at Georgia Tech, where he averaged 23 points a game, Anderson decided to turn pro. The Nets made him No. 2 overall in the 1991 Draft. As a rookie in 1991-92, he and then-coach Bill Fitch didn't always see eye to eye. Anderson gathered a lot of splinters on the bench.

But it all turned around in 1992-93 when Daly became coach and Anderson shined as a penetrator and ball-handler. Then came the first broken wrist.

In 1993-94, Anderson was at his best with 9.6 assists per game for No. 4 in the NBA and an 18.8 scoring average that topped all point guards in the league. And he was chosen a starter in the All-Star Game.

His goals: No more wrist problems and, of course, a title for the Nets.

Year	Team	G	FG	FG Pct.	FT	FT Pct.	Reb.	Ast.	TP	Avg.
1991-92	New Jersey	64	187	.390	73	.745	127	203	450	7.0
1992-93	New Jersey	55	370	.435	180	.776	226	449	927	16.9
1993-94	New Jersey	82	576	.417	346	.818	322	784	1538	18.8
	Totals	201	1133	.418	599	.795	675	1436	2915	14.5
	Playoff Totals	7	22	.349	24	.686	15	30	71	10.1

JIM JACKSON
"Dr. J" in the Making

"He did things with the ball that I couldn't believe," said Jim Jackson of his boyhood hero, Julius Erving, known as "Dr. J."

In a few years, some aspiring basketball player may be saying the same of the Dallas Mavericks' shooting guard. In his first full season, the 6'6", 220-pound Jackson averaged 19.2 points, tying him for 18th with teammate Jamal Mashburn in NBA scoring.

Born October 14, 1970, in Toledo, Ohio, Jackson has been a super athlete at every level. He twice took Macomber High School to the state championship and was selected as Ohio's "Mr. Basketball." He first dunked a ball as a 6'3" seventh-grader. And he caught 14 TD passes as a Macomber football player.

But it was all basketball for him at Ohio State, where he led the Buckeyes to three straight NCAA tournament appearances and back-to-back titles in the Big Ten. After his All-American junior season, his last at Ohio State, he played for the U.S. team that won a bronze medal in the Pan American Games.

Selected by the Mavs with the fourth pick in the 1992 NBA Draft, a lengthy holdout limited him to only 28 games as a rookie. In 1993-94, he started every game, displaying his special passing and rebounding skills, and ability to score from anywhere.

Year	Team	G	FG	FG Pct.	FT	FT Pct.	Reb.	Ast.	TP	Avg.
1992-93	Dallas	28	184	.395	68	.739	122	131	457	16.3
1993-94	Dallas	82	637	.445	285	.821	388	374	1576	19.2
	Totals	110	821	.433	353	.804	510	505	2033	18.5

JAMAL MASHBURN
"The Mash" Is a Smash

"He's the most well-rounded rookie I've seen this year," said Detroit's Joe Dumars during the 1993-94 season.

Dumars wasn't referring to the 240 pounds the 6'8" Jamal Mashburn brings into play as an outstanding forward with the Dallas Mavericks.

Mashburn averaged 19.2 points and made the All-Rookie team along with such other rising stars as Golden State's Chris Webber (now with Washington) and Orlando's Anfernee Hardaway.

"He's hard to play against because he's so versatile," said the Phoenix Suns' Charles Barkley. "He has the game of a forward but the skills of a guard. He can beat you in a lot of different ways."

Anyone who knew of Mashburn as a youngster in New York City, where he was born November 29, 1972, expected nothing less. He first gained attention when he led Cardinal Hayes High School to its first city championship in 50 years. He developed his game playing in the famed Rucker League, where such immortals as Julius Erving and Connie Hawkins had distinguished themselves.

Mashburn was an All-American at the University of Kentucky, pacing the Wildcats to two consecutive Southeastern Conference titles and the NCAA Final Four in 1993. He left school after his junior year, and the Mavs chose him No. 4 overall in the 1993 NBA Draft.

An instant success in the pros, Mashburn made the All-Rookie team and now there's a line of sneakers named for him called "The Mash."

Year	Team	G	FG	FG Pct.	FT	FT Pct.	Reb.	Ast.	TP	Avg.
1993-94	Dallas	79	561	.406	306	.699	353	266	1513	19.2

SHAWN KEMP
Skipping to the Pros

He took an unusual route to the NBA. He never played a minute of college basketball.

Somehow there were enough scouting reports based on Shawn Kemp's high school play to inspire the Seattle SuperSonics to select him as a 19-year-old in the 1989 NBA Draft. And there are no regrets.

The 6'10", 245-pound forward has become one of the mainstays of a franchise that won more games (63) than any other team in 1993-94. "He's the key to our team," said SuperSonic coach George Karl.

Kemp has done it with his shot-blocking, rebounding, and scoring. For the fourth straight season, he has led the Sonics in blocked shots and rebounding, and he was their top shooter (18.1) in 1993-94.

He is known for his sensational dunks—he was second to the Boston Celtics' Dee Brown in the 1991 Slam-Dunk competition at All-Star Weekend.

Kemp has played in the last two All-Star Games and on USA Dream Team II.

Five years in the NBA and he's only beginning. Phoenix Suns coach Paul Westphal said, "Kemp has only scratched the surface."

What's he going to be like when he grows up?

Year	Team	G	FG	FG Pct.	FT	FT Pct.	Reb.	Ast.	TP	Avg.
1989-90	Seattle	81	203	.479	117	.736	346	26	525	6.5
1990-91	Seattle	81	462	.508	288	.661	679	144	1214	15.0
1991-92	Seattle	64	362	.504	270	.748	665	86	994	15.5
1992-93	Seattle	78	515	.492	358	.712	833	155	1388	17.8
1993-94	Seattle	79	533	.538	364	.741	851	207	1431	18.1
Totals		383	2075	.508	1397	.716	3374	618	5552	14.5
Playoff Totals		38	206	.465	198	.776	385	76	610	16.1

JOHN STARKS
From Supermarket to Superstar

The banner in Chicago Stadium read: "Hey, Starks: Price Check in Aisle 6."

John Starks could laugh at the sign unfurled near halfcourt. It wasn't so long ago that he was checking prices and bagging groceries in a supermarket. Nowadays, as a star guard for the New York Knicks, he no longer has to ask customers if they want paper or plastic bags.

With his supermarket days behind him, Starks has blossomed to where he was selected to his first All-Star Game in 1993-94 and played a key role in the Knicks' first trip to the NBA Finals in 21 years.

"John is a very dangerous player," said Houston Rockets coach Rudy Tomjanovich. "In terms of getting his shot off, he's one of the quickest players in the league. You think you're on him, but all he needs is a split-second and he can get it off and in the basket."

The 6'5", 185-pound Stark's route to the heights of the NBA has been less than direct. Born August 10, 1965, in Tulsa, Oklahoma, he played only a season of high-school ball and attended four state colleges in four years, finishing at Oklahoma State.

He never was drafted by an NBA team, but signed as a free agent with the Golden State Warriors in 1989. He was released after 36 games and landed in the Continental Basketball Association, playing in Cedar Rapids, Iowa.

The Knicks signed him as a free agent at the start of the 1990-91 season and he finally found his niche in the big league as a player who never backs down from anything, can take the clutch shot, and be a tenacious defender.

Starks tore cartilage in his left knee and missed the last 23 games of the 1993-94 season. After surgery, he came back in time for the playoffs that would spotlight him forever.

He was sensational in Game 6 of the NBA Finals against Houston, scoring 16 points in a fourth-quarter comeback. But his potential game-winning 3-point attempt was blocked by Hakeem Olajuwon, sending the series to Game 7. Sadly, in the most important game of his life, he wound up shooting 2-for-18 as Houston captured the championship.

There were critics who felt Knicks coach Pat Riley should have benched Starks as he kept missing shot after shot. To that, Riley responded: "You go up with your players and you go down with them. John is fearless. He is one of the great competitors I've been around in my life. He's a tough kid and he'll eventually be able to lick his wounds, get over it, and learn from it."

After 4 seasons in New York, Starks already ranks second in team history in 3-point makes. This turns out to be very profitable for the Boys Brotherhood Republic. Starks donates $100 to that organization every time he cans a trey at Madison Square Garden.

Year	Team	G	FG	FG Pct.	FT	FT Pct.	Reb.	Ast.	TP	Avg.
1988-89	Golden State	36	51	.408	34	.654	41	27	146	4.1
1990-91	New York	61	180	.439	79	.752	131	204	466	7.6
1991-92	New York	82	405	.449	235	.778	191	276	1139	13.9
1992-93	New York	80	513	.428	263	.795	204	404	1397	17.5
1993-94	New York	59	410	.420	187	.754	185	348	1120	19.0
	Totals	318	1559	.431	798	.769	752	1259	4268	13.4
	Playoff Totals	55	246	.399	184	.767	143	254	762	13.9

RON HARPER
A New Bull

Ron Harper still remembers the day he was cut from his freshman team in high school. He was hurt and embarrassed, but used the setback in a positive way.

"I decided at that point that nothing was going to stop me," said Harper. "That made me even more determined to succeed in basketball."

The 6'6", 198-pound guard shines as a symbol of determination. He's had much to overcome along the way. For one, he had a severe speech impediment that caused him to stutter. As a pro, Harper had to overcome a career-threatening knee injury in 1990.

The youngest of six children, Harper was born January 20, 1964, in Dayton, Ohio, where he grew up playing basketball. His mother, Gloretha, put up the Harpers' first hoop in their backyard.

He was an outstanding player at Kiser High and went on to Miami of Ohio, where he was the school's all-time leading scorer and a fearsome rebounding guard in the Mid-American Conference.

The Cleveland Cavaliers drafted him eighth overall in 1986 and he was an instant hero. He led the team in scoring (22.9), made the All-Rookie team, and finished runner-up to Indiana's Chuck Person for Rookie of the Year honors.

Early in the 1989-90 season, the Cavs traded him to the Clippers for Reggie Williams and the rights to Danny Ferry. But then came the knee injury that could have put an end to his trademark drives and dunks.

But Harper made it all the way back. In 1993-94, he had one of his finest all-around seasons with 20.1 points per game for 15th in the NBA. And late in the summer of 1994 he signed as a free agent with the Chicago Bulls.

Year	Team	G	FG	FG Pct.	FT	FT Pct.	Reb.	Ast.	TP	Avg.
1986-87	Cleveland	82	734	.455	386	.684	392	394	1874	22.9
1987-88	Cleveland	57	340	.464	196	.705	223	281	879	15.4
1988-89	Cleveland	82	587	.511	323	.751	409	434	1526	18.6
1989-90	Clev.-LAC	35	301	.473	182	.788	206	182	798	22.8
1990-91	L.A. Clippers	39	285	.391	145	.668	188	209	763	19.6
1991-92	L.A. Clippers	82	569	.440	293	.736	447	417	1495	18.2
1992-93	L.A. Clippers	80	542	.451	307	.769	425	360	1443	18.0
1993-94	L.A. Clippers	75	569	.426	299	.715	460	344	1508	20.1
	Totals	532	3927	.452	2131	.726	2750	2621	10286	19.3
	Playoff Totals	19	145	.488	53	.726	93	74	349	18.4

OTIS THORPE
Unforgettable Rocket

In one of their losses to the New York Knicks in the 1993-94 NBA Finals, the Houston Rockets' Otis Thorpe got off only three shots.

So before the next game, coach Rudy Tomjanovich wrote on the lockerroom blackboard: "Don't forget OT."

"This was unusual for me," Tomjanovich said. "I almost never write messages about players on the blackboard. In this case I had to. You just can't forget someone like Otis."

From then on, the Rockets didn't forget him. Thorpe responded, winding up with 27-for-53 for a .519 percentage, second only to teammate Carl Herrera's .579, as the Rockets took the championship.

The 6'10", 246-pound forward's performance came as no surprise. No. 3 in NBA regular-season shooting percentage in 1993-94, Thorpe has ranked among the top five in each of the last three seasons. A strong rebounder as well, he finished 15th in the league in that department in the title season.

The third youngest of 11 children, he was born August 5, 1962, in Boynton Beach, Florida. He was a late starter in high school, where he played only a year-and-half before enrolling at Providence College. There he finished as the Big East's career leader in rebounds and was second in scoring to Chris Mullin of St. John's.

"At first I hadn't really thought about playing pro ball," he said. "I was concentrating on graduating and getting into some kind of work. Then in my junior year I felt I could probably play in the NBA."

The ninth overall pick by the Kansas City (now

Sacramento) Kings in 1984, he soon became known as one of basketball's iron men. Except for 1985-86, when he suffered a bruised kidney, and 1992-93, he has played in every game during his 10-year career. The Rockets made a winning deal when they got him in a trade for Rodney McCray and Jim Petersen in 1988.

"When you get the ball to Otis, he's either going to score or make the pass that will get you a basket," said Thorpe's teammate Kenny Smith.

Overshadowed by Hakeem Olajuwon, Thorpe doesn't get as many headlines, but the Rockets and their opponents know he's one player nobody dares to ignore.

Year	Team	G	FG	FG Pct.	FT	FT Pct.	Reb.	Ast.	TP	Avg.
1984-85	Kansas City	82	411	.600	230	.620	556	111	1052	12.8
1985-86	Sacramento	75	289	.587	164	.661	420	84	742	9.9
1986-87	Sacramento	82	567	.540	413	.761	819	201	1547	18.9
1987-88	Sacramento	82	622	.507	460	.755	837	266	1704	20.8
1988-89	Houston	82	521	.542	328	.729	787	202	1370	16.7
1989-90	Houston	82	547	.548	307	.688	734	261	1401	17.1
1990-91	Houston	82	549	.556	334	.696	846	197	1435	17.5
1991-92	Houston	82	558	.592	304	.657	862	250	1420	17.3
1992-93	Houston	72	385	.558	153	.598	589	181	923	12.8
1993-94	Houston	82	449	.561	251	.657	870	189	1149	14.0
Totals		803	4898	.554	2944	.693	7320	1942	12743	15.9
Playoff Totals		49	260	.588	117	.622	421	112	638	13.0

GARY PAYTON
A Sonic Boom

When you watch Gary Payton play, you can't help but hear him. He's the one constantly talking to and harassing opponents. The SuperSonics' point guard simply can't let his action speak for itself.

"That's how I played when I grew up," he said. "I can't

be as effective if I don't play the game my way. If someone put a muzzle on me, I couldn't be the same player."

And that obviously would be a mistake. In a very short time, Payton has developed into one of the premier defensive players in the NBA. In 1993-94, only his fourth season in the league, he was voted onto the NBA All-Defensive First Team and made his first All-Star Game team.

The 6'4", 190-pound Payton was fourth in the NBA in steals, improving by five spots his ninth-place ranking from a season before. In addition, his ability to consistently hit from the outside, long a weak spot in his game, was a key factor in his team's performance as the SuperSonics won a team-record 63 games with him spearheading their pressing, scrambling style.

"So much of what we do starts with Gary," said Seattle coach George Karl. "He can shut other guys down or make them really work to dribble the ball up the floor."

Born July 23, 1968, in Oakland, California, he grew up rooting for the Oakland A's and was a shortstop at Skyline High School, as well as a leading man on the basketball team.

He became Oregon State's all-time leading scorer and was second on the all-time NCAA lists in steals and assists. As a senior in 1989-90, he was named Pac-10 Player of the Year and was *Sports Illustrated's* College Player of the Year. The SuperSonics drafted him with the second pick overall in 1990, making him the highest draft pick in Seattle history.

Payton uses his long arms and quickness to hound opponents. And he has missed only one game in four seasons.

The Sonic who has worn No. 20 since he was in fourth grade has proved he's more than all talk.

Year	Team	G	FG	FG Pct.	FT	FT Pct.	Reb.	Ast.	TP	Avg.
1990-91	Seattle	82	259	.450	69	.711	243	528	588	7.2
1991-92	Seattle	81	331	.451	99	.669	295	506	764	9.4
1992-93	Seattle	82	476	.494	151	.770	281	399	1110	13.5
1993-94	Seattle	82	584	.504	166	.595	269	494	1349	16.5
	Totals	327	1650	.481	485	.674	1088	1927	3811	11.7
	Playoff Totals	37	176	.452	42	.600	114	168	398	10.8

GLEN RICE
Turning Up the Heat

If Glen Rice could change one thing, it would be his hands. They're so small, he's one of the very few NBA players who can't palm the basketball.

"I've always thought my hands were too small," Rice said. "If I could palm the basketball, I could do a lot more when I go to the basket."

Even with his small hands, Rice can do plenty right now. He's one of the best shooters in the game. The 6'8", 200-pound forward, fourth pick overall in the 1989 Draft, has been the Miami Heat's leading scorer for three years and is the team's top 3-point shooter. He has made at least 130 treys three straight years.

"Glen has a star's mentality and charisma," said Heat coach Kevin Loughery. "He's one of those guys who can shoot the ball. He can shoot the three. And that's what fans are looking for. They want to see players dunk, shoot the 3-point shot, block shots, or make the great pass. Glen can do all of that."

Born May 28, 1967, in Flint, Michigan, he was Mr. Basketball in the state as a schoolboy. He led Michigan to the NCAA title in 1989. In the championship game against Seton Hall, he scored 31 points and grabbed 11 rebounds. For his accomplishments, he won the Jesse Owens award that goes to the top athlete in the Big Ten in any sport. When he left the Wolverines, he was the Big Ten's all-time leading scorer.

"You can never let Glen get free," said Cleveland Cavs coach Mike Fratello. "He'll kill you with his long-range shots. He's the one guy we always pay attention to."

Little hands and all.

Year	Team	G	FG	FG Pct.	FT	FT Pct.	Reb.	Ast.	TP	Avg.
1989-90	Miami	77	470	.439	91	.734	352	138	1048	13.6
1990-91	Miami	77	550	.461	171	.818	381	189	1342	17.4
1991-92	Miami	79	672	.469	266	.836	394	184	1765	22.3
1992-93	Miami	82	582	.440	242	.820	424	180	1554	19.0
1993-94	Miami	81	663	.467	250	.880	434	184	1708	21.1
	Totals	396	2937	.456	1020	.829	1985	875	7417	18.7
	Playoff Totals	8	50	.379	12	.800	46	15	122	15.3

CHARLES OAKLEY
A Man for All Seasons

Known for his all-out play and hustle, Charles Oakley is, in the words of one of his Knicks teammates, "the glue to our team. No one works harder."

That means on and off the court. Need a magnificent rebounder? Someone to fetch loose balls? A mid-range face-up jumper? Or how 'bout a car wash?

In the summer, Oakley can be found putting on gloves and boots and helping out at his car wash in Cleveland, Ohio.

"I don't know why, but my son just always loved to wash cars," said Corine Oakley, Charles' mom. "Even when he was a little boy."

Coach Pat Riley regards him as "the best defensive forward in the game." This bruising 6'9", 245-pounder does it with bulk, strength, and desire, and he hasn't missed a game in the past two seasons. This despite aches and pains that are the result of bruises and sprains.

Born December 18, 1963, in Cleveland, he played at a small college, Virginia Union. But that didn't keep him from being selected with the ninth pick of the 1985 Draft. He started his career in Chicago and was traded to the Knicks for Bill Cartwright in 1988.

In 1993-94, he was selected to the NBA's All-Defensive First Team for the first time. He finished tied with Denver's Dikembe Mutumbo for sixth in rebounding with an 11.8 average. He helped lead the Knicks to their first NBA Finals in 21 years.

"I'm just glad I'm being recognized for the kind of player I am," he said. "I play a position where the guys don't get the recognition we deserve. I'm not the great scorer. But I contribute in my own way."

"We wouldn't be where we are today without Charles," said Riley. "His dedication to work is something to which all players should aspire."

Year	Team	G	FG	FG Pct.	FT	FT Pct.	Reb.	Ast.	TP	Avg.
1985-86	Chicago	77	281	.519	178	.662	664	133	740	9.6
1986-87	Chicago	82	468	.445	245	.686	1074	296	1192	14.5
1987-88	Chicago	82	375	.483	261	.727	1066	248	1014	12.4
1988-89	New York	82	426	.510	197	.773	861	187	1061	12.9
1989-90	New York	61	336	.524	217	.761	727	146	889	14.6
1990-91	New York	76	307	.516	239	.784	920	204	853	11.2
1991-92	New York	82	210	.522	86	.735	700	133	506	6.2
1992-93	New York	82	219	.508	127	.722	708	126	565	6.9
1993-94	New York	82	363	.478	243	.776	965	218	969	11.8
Totals		706	2985	.495	1793	.736	7685	1691	7789	11.0
Playoff Totals		90	368	.465	241	.737	1011	166	981	10.9

VERNON MAXWELL
"Mad Max"

If there's one NBA player who lives up to his nickname, it is the Houston Rockets' Vernon Maxwell. They call him "Mad Max."

Maxwell, a 6'4", 190-pound shooting guard, often yells at teammates and challenges opponents to their faces. He sometimes gets into arguments with officials, occasionally getting hit with technical fouls.

"Off the court, I want to be known as Vernon Maxwell," he says. "But when I'm on the floor playing, I don't mind people calling me 'Mad Max.' I can't play with all those emotions bottled up inside me. I've got to let them out."

Maxwell also lets fly in the literal sense. He is one of the game's most dangerous shooters, and is only 1 of 13 players in NBA history to make 500 3-pointers in his career.

He canned four 3-pointers in one quarter of Game 5 of the Western Conference Finals against Utah in 1993-94. But his biggest shot ever was a 3-pointer that assured the Game 7 victory over New York for the 1994 NBA title. More than a scorer, he led the Rockets in assists and steals, and was a defensive ace in their championship season. He once scored 51 points, against Cleveland in 1991.

He was Florida's all-time scoring leader with 2,450 points and was second in Southeastern Conference history to Louisiana State's "Pistol Pete" Maravich. Known as "Hawk" in high school, he grew up four miles from the Florida campus. Maxwell was the state's Mr. Basketball as a high school senior, and he made All-

State as a defensive back in football.

He was born September 12, 1965, in Gainesville, Florida. Despite his college achievements, he didn't become a star overnight in the NBA. Originally drafted as a second-rounder by Denver in 1988, he was traded on draft day to San Antonio. The Rockets paid $50,000 to obtain him from the Spurs during the 1989-90 season and he blossomed thereafter.

Year	Team	G	FG	FG Pct.	FT	FT Pct.	Reb.	Ast.	TP	Avg.
1988-89	San Antonio	79	357	.432	181	.745	202	301	927	11.7
1989-90	S.A.-Houston	79	275	.439	136	.645	228	296	714	9.0
1990-91	Houston	82	504	.404	217	.733	238	303	1397	17.0
1991-92	Houston	80	502	.413	206	.772	243	326	1372	17.2
1992-93	Houston	71	349	.407	164	.719	221	297	982	13.8
1993-94	Houston	75	380	.389	143	.749	229	380	1023	13.6
	Totals	466	2367	.412	1047	.729	1361	1903	6415	13.8
	Playoff Totals	39	218	.384	70	.693	123	154	579	14.8

LATRELL SPREWELL
Almost Out of Nowhere

More than a few people were surprised when the Golden State Warriors took Latrell Sprewell with the 24th pick in the 1992 NBA Draft. He was a fine defensive player at Alabama, but not the center the Warriors needed.

But in only his second season, 1993-94, the 6'5", 195-pound guard was named to the All-NBA First Team.

"He was the steal of the draft," said former Kings general manager Jerry Reynolds.

"Spree" earned his berth with a spectacular offensive game, including 3-pointers and defense. His

21 points a game made him 11th in the league, his 2.20 steals were ninth-best, and no guard had more blocks.

"He's incredible and he's all ours," said coach Don Nelson. "He gets better all the time. He absorbs everything you give him. We're thrilled."

Sprewell was born September 8, 1970, in Milwaukee, Wisconsin. He didn't play high school ball until his senior year at Washington High and he also competed in the long jump and triple jump.

He played two years at Three Rivers Community College in Poplar Bluff, Missouri, before moving on to Alabama, where he was overshadowed by teammate Robert Horry, now with the Houston Rockets. But he wound up on the All-Southeastern Conference first team with such other 1992 first-round draft picks as Shaq O'Neal, Lee Mayberry, and Horry.

As a rookie, he was fifth among NBA rookies in scoring, first in 3-point shooting and assists, and second in steals. Indeed, he was the No. 1 steal for the Warriors.

Year	Team	G	FG	FG Pct.	FT	FT Pct.	Reb.	Ast.	TP	Avg.
1992-93	Golden State	77	449	.464	211	.746	271	295	1182	15.4
1993-94	Golden State	82	613	.433	353	.774	401	385	1720	21.0
	Totals	159	1062	.445	564	.763	672	680	2902	18.3
Playoff Totals		3	26	.433	8	.667	9	21	68	22.7

CHRIS MULLIN
Winning When It Matters

When Chris Mullin stood on the trophy platform at the 1992 Olympic Games in Barcelona, Spain, he completed a rare double. The Dream Team member became only the sixth player in Olympic basketball history to win two gold medals. His first came in 1984 in Los Angeles.

In the years between the Games and after, his has been a story of courage and comeback. Mullin has had to face a variety of setbacks and tragedies, including the death of his dad, Rod, in 1992 and mother, Eileen, in 1993. Heading into his tenth season as a Golden State Warrior in 1994-95, the 6'7", 215-pound forward remains, as Warriors coach Don Nelson says, "a truly remarkable performer."

Until last season, he had led the Warriors in scoring for six consecutive years, the last of which (1992-93) was marred by a thumb injury that caused Mullin to miss 36 games. More surgery for torn ligaments in his right hand hampered him in 1993-94, but he gamely played on.

"He's so smart," said San Antonio's Sean Elliott, who had many one-on-ones with him. "He knows how to use screens as well as anyone."

Born July 30, 1963, in Brooklyn, New York, he displayed a feathery touch as a shooter from his earliest days. Known as a gym rat because he would practice for endless hours, Mullin won the John Wooden Award as the nation's top collegian at St. John's in 1985.

Golden State took him as the seventh pick in the 1985 NBA Draft. He made the All-NBA First Team in 1992, the Second Team in 1989 and 1991, and the Third Team in 1990. And he has been an All-Star Game selection six times.

Early in his pro career, he acknowledged his alcohol addiction and sought help to overcome the problem. He has been sober ever since.

Year	Team	G	FG	FG Pct.	FT	FT Pct.	Reb.	Ast.	TP	Avg.
1985-86	Golden State	55	287	.463	189	.896	115	105	768	14.0
1986-87	Golden State	82	477	.514	269	.825	181	261	1242	15.1
1987-88	Golden State	60	470	.508	239	.885	205	290	1213	20.2
1988-89	Golden State	82	830	.509	493	.892	483	415	2176	26.5
1989-90	Golden State	78	682	.536	505	.889	463	319	1956	25.1
1990-91	Golden State	82	777	.536	513	.884	443	329	2107	25.7
1991-92	Golden State	81	830	.524	350	.833	450	286	2074	25.6
1992-93	Golden State	46	474	.510	183	.810	232	166	1191	25.9
1993-94	Golden State	62	410	.472	165	.753	345	315	1040	16.8
	Totals	628	5237	.513	2906	.862	2917	2486	13767	21.9
	Playoff Totals	33	263	.520	136	.861	146	105	685	20.8

STEVE SMITH
At Home With His Hoops

You walk into the Smiths' backyard in Detroit and immediately you spot the basketball court and hoop. But neither the backboard nor the rim is the same as those that Steve Smith shot at when he was growing up.

"That's the third backboard and the 15th rim we've had up there," proudly says the Atlanta Hawks' 6'8", 213-pound guard.

The Smiths' court was the neighborhood playground. It was built by his father, Donald, now a retired bus driver. Dozens of kids would converge on the court and stand in line awaiting their turn to play. It went on every day until dark. And it was here that Smith started on the road to the pros.

Born March 31, 1969, in Highland Park, Michigan, he went from high school standout to Big Ten star at Michigan State. He led the Spartans in scoring three straight seasons and, as a senior, he made All-Big Ten.

Drafted by the Miami Heat with the 11th pick

overall in 1991, he missed 55 games in his first two seasons because of knee injuries. But in 1993-94, he played in all but four games, was second in scoring to Glen Rice, and was selected for USA Dream Team II. In the first week of the 1994-95 season, he was traded with Grant Long to Atlanta for Kevin Willis.

His father was the "commissioner" of their backyard league, but his mother, Belle, had to put up with the endless basketball. That's one reason Smith wears sneakers with the name "Belle" sewn into the sides.

Whenever he returns home, Smith still takes his shots in the old backyard and he also works on the antique cars that he collects with his boyhood pal, Derrick Coleman of the New Jersey Nets. They like to rebuild classic cars and then park them next to the court. His favorite is a yellow 1957 Chevy.

Year	Team	G	FG	FG Pct.	FT	FT Pct.	Reb.	Ast.	TP	Avg.
1991-92	Miami	61	297	.454	95	.748	188	278	729	12.0
1992-93	Miami	48	279	.451	155	.787	197	267	766	16.0
1993-94	Miami	78	491	.456	273	.835	352	394	1346	17.3
	Totals	187	1067	.454	523	.803	737	939	2841	15.2
Playoff Totals		8	51	.447	26	.839	36	26	144	18.0

DANNY MANNING
All in the Family

Ed Manning played nine seasons with six teams in the NBA and the long-gone ABA. "Wait 'til you see my son, Danny," Ed used to say. "He'll make the Mannings famous."

Danny began fulfilling dad's prediction at Kansas, where he was MVP of the 1988 NCAA tourney as he led the Jayhawks to the championship. But it has been a slower journey in the NBA.

The Los Angeles Clippers tagged him as the first pick in the 1988 Draft. A 6'10", 234-pound forward, he came in labeled as one who could dribble like a playmaker, shoot from the outside like a shooting guard, and rebound like a power forward.

But Manning's career was sidetracked after only 26 games as a rookie when he tore a ligament in his right knee after a fast-break layup. That ended his season. It's a tribute to his work ethic that he eventually regained his form. In 1991-92, he played in every game and led the Clippers in scoring.

His real breakthrough year came in 1992-93 when he set a Clipper record for points and field goals and became the first Clipper selected for the All-Star Game since Marques Johnson in 1986.

Traded during the 1993-94 season to the Atlanta Hawks in a deal that brought Dominique Wilkins to the Clippers, Manning ended up leading the Hawks in playoff scoring.

But he wouldn't be a Hawk for long. An unrestricted free agent, he signed with the Phoenix Suns in the summer of '94. And now he'll try to make the Mannings even more famous.

Year	Team	G	FG	FG Pct.	FT	FT Pct.	Reb.	Ast.	TP	Avg.
1988-89	L.A. Clippers	26	177	.494	79	.767	171	81	434	16.7
1989-90	L.A. Clippers	71	440	.533	274	.741	422	187	1154	16.3
1990-91	L.A. Clippers	73	470	.519	219	.716	426	196	1159	15.9
1991-92	L.A. Clippers	82	650	.542	279	.725	564	285	1579	19.3
1992-93	L.A. Clippers	79	702	.509	388	.802	520	207	1800	22.8
1993-94	L.A. Clippers	68	586	.488	228	.669	465	261	1403	20.6
	Totals	399	3025	.516	1467	.738	2568	1217	7529	18.9
	Playoff Totals	21	165	.488	93	.756	141	59	424	20.2

CLIFFORD ROBINSON
"So I Won't Quarterback"

Growing up in Buffalo, New York, Clifford Robinson's earliest goal was to one day be the quarterback of the Buffalo Bills. He was the signal-caller for his junior varsity team at Riverside High School. But he soon got so tall, the only sport for him was basketball.

Rated one of the top schoolboy prospects in the nation, he became a leading scorer and rebounder at the University of Connecticut. But that didn't assure a role in the NBA for the 6'10", 225-pound forward-center.

Robinson didn't get taken until the second round (No. 36) in the 1989 NBA Draft and played mostly in reserve roles. "I just kept working hard and believing in myself," he said.

He was finally recognized for his all-around performance in 1992-93, when the NBA named him Sixth Man of the Year. The following year, Robinson started 61 games at center and his 20.1 points made him No. 1 on the team and No. 15 in the league. He also played in his first All-Star Game.

"Few guys Cliff's size can get up and down the floor like he can," said teammate Clyde Drexler. "Cliff's got a world of athletic ability."

He is also a model of endurance. In his 5-year career, he has never missed a game.

Robinson was born December 16, 1966, in Albion, New York, and has a sister, Alisa, who played basketball at Canisius College in Buffalo.

The family can't root for him as quarterback of the

Bills, but they sure follow his every box score as the emerging star of the Trail Blazers.

Year	Team	G	FG	FG Pct.	FT	FT Pct.	Reb.	Ast.	TP	Avg.
1989-90	Portland...............	82	298	.397	138	.550	308	72	746	9.1
1990-91	Portland...............	82	373	.463	205	.653	349	151	957	11.7
1991-92	Portland...............	82	396	.466	219	.664	416	137	1016	12.4
1992-93	Portland...............	82	632	.473	287	.690	542	182	1570	19.1
1993-94	Portland...............	82	641	.457	352	.765	550	159	1647	20.1
	Totals	410	2342	.455	1201	.678	2165	701	5936	14.5
	Playoff Totals........................	66	252	.424	127	.557	280	100	635	9.6

CHRISTIAN LAETTNER
Stepping Up From the Dream Team

Christian Laettner was named for Christian Diestl, a German soldier played by Marlon Brando in the film *The Young Lions*. That title sums up the Minnesota Timber-wolves' power forward.

The young lion in a wolf's uniform, Laettner was the player chosen third overall in the 1992 NBA Draft in the hope he would lead Minnesota out of the wilderness.

The 6'11", 235-pounder came into the league with a winning history. An All-American and a 4-year starter at Duke, he led the Blue Devils to consecutive NCAA titles in 1991 and 1992.

It was also in 1992 that Laettner enjoyed the unique experience of playing with Michael Jordan, Magic Johnson, Larry Bird, and the other pro superstars in the Olympic Games at Barcelona, Spain. The only collegian on the squad, he was a member of the Dream Team that won the gold medal. What a way to prepare for a career in the NBA!

Laettner averaged 18.2 points and made the NBA All-Rookie Team in 1992-93. He made an instant impression as a demanding player. But that's because he wants to win so badly. "I came here to help the Timberwolves build a champion. That's how I play," he said.

He's proved tough for opposing power forwards to handle because he can battle inside or score from the outside. And he's a precision passer.

Born August 17, 1969, in Angola, New York, Laettner starred at Nichols School in Buffalo. He has a brother, Chris, who is a minor-league umpire in baseball.

Year	Team	G	FG	FG Pct.	FT	FT Pct.	Reb.	Ast.	TP	Avg.
1992-93	Minnesota	81	503	.474	462	.835	708	223	1472	18.2
1993-94	Minnesota	70	396	.448	375	.783	602	307	1173	16.8
	Totals	151	899	.462	837	.811	1310	530	2645	17.5

DERRICK COLEMAN
Net Gain

As the tape of the New Jersey-Charlotte game played in the Nets' locker room, Derrick Coleman provided the play-by-play commentary. He did a perfect imitation of TV analyst Bill Raftery.

"Bill has heard me do him and thinks it's pretty good," Coleman said. "When it comes to doing sportscasters, I can imitate a few of them."

But few NBA players can imitate Coleman, the enormously talented power forward of the Nets. Inside, the 6'10", 235-pounder can outmuscle most opponents for baskets. Outside, he has 3-point range. He can dominate the defensive boards and is quick enough to run the break. "With the exception of Utah's Karl Malone, I don't think there's a better power forward in the game," said Coleman's new coach, Butch Beard. "Derrick can do everything."

Coleman averaged 20 points and 10 rebounds for the second straight season in 1993-94 and emerged as the team leader in his most consistent season. And he was a starter in the All-Star Game.

Born June 21, 1967, in Mobile, Alabama, Coleman grew up in Detroit and attended Syracuse. He was a 4-year starter, and when he left, he was the first player in NCAA history to have recorded at least 2,000 points, 1,500 rebounds, and 300 blocks.

He was the No. 1 pick in the 1990 Draft, and was Rookie of the Year in 1990-91 when he led all rookies in scoring. Coleman played for USA Dream Team II in 1994.

Year	Team	G	FG	FG Pct.	FT	FT Pct.	Reb.	Ast.	TP	Avg.
1990-91	New Jersey	74	514	.467	323	.731	759	163	1364	18.4
1991-92	New Jersey	65	483	.504	300	.763	618	205	1289	19.8
1992-93	New Jersey	76	564	.460	421	.808	852	276	1572	20.7
1993-94	New Jersey	77	541	.447	439	.774	870	262	1559	20.2
Totals		292	2102	.468	1483	.771	3099	906	5784	19.8
Playoff Totals		13	113	.479	84	.785	169	54	321	24.7

ANFERNEE HARDAWAY
A Penny Worth a Fortune

Louise Hardaway called her grandson "Pretty" when young Anfernee was just a toddler. But something got lost in the translation.

"All my friends thought she was calling me 'Penny,'" said Hardaway. "That's why they call me 'Penny.'"

By any name, Hardaway has made a name for himself after just a season in the NBA. Taking a leadership role with the Orlando Magic, he teamed with Shaquille O'Neal to spark the Magic to its first 50-win season and first berth in the playoffs in 1993-94.

The 6'7", 195-pound guard led all rookies in steals and assists. An excellent passer and defender, he made the All-Rookie Team, narrowly missing out as Rookie of the Year to the Golden State Warriors' Chris Webber.

"At times I thought I was looking in the mirror," said Magic Johnson. "He reminds me so much of myself."

That's high praise, indeed, from the former Los Angeles Laker superstar who won five NBA championships with the Lakers and retired as the league's all-time assist leader.

Hardaway, who was born July 18, 1972, in Memphis, Tennessee, was an only child raised by his grandmother. "I owe so much to her," he said. "She taught me the difference between right and wrong. She kept me healthy and well-fed."

He starred at Treadwell High in Memphis and enrolled at Memphis State. As a freshman, he had to sit out the season because of poor grades. Worse still, he and a friend were robbed at gunpoint. When Hardaway dove for cover, he was shot in the right foot, fracturing three bones.

"At that time, I was lazy," he said. "I had no drive. No motivation. But after I got shot, that changed all of that. I realized what I was doing to myself. It was a real wake-up call."

He went on to a glorious career at Memphis State, where they saluted him by retiring his No. 25. He was selected by the Warriors with the third pick in the 1993 Draft. But on draft day, Golden State, loaded with talent in the back-court, sought help in the frontcourt and traded Hardaway to the Magic in exchange for No. 1 pick Chris Webber.

The deal may have meant a lot to the Warriors, but this "Penny" was worth a fortune to the Magic.

Year	Team	G	FG	FG Pct.	FT	FT Pct.	Reb.	Ast.	TP	Avg.
1993-94	Orlando	82	509	.466	245	.742	439	544	1313	16.0
Playoff Totals		3	22	.440	7	.700	20	21	56	18.7

TIM HARDAWAY
One Mighty Bug

"Tim Bug," as his teammates call him, was at the top of his game in 1992-93 when he became the fifth player in NBA history to average 20 points and 10 assists in consecutive seasons. That put him in the rare company of Oscar Robert-son, Magic Johnson, Isiah Thomas, and Kevin Johnson.

But Tim Hardaway injured his right knee late in the season, causing him to miss 16 games, and then he tore a ligament in his left knee in training camp in 1993. He missed the entire 1993-94 season and now, after extensive rehabilitation, he has resumed his brilliant career.

His crossover dribble, cat-quick first step to the hoop, shooting skills, and floor play have made him one of the best point guards in the game.

Stronger than most small guards, the sturdily built 6-foot, 195-pounder is treasured for his power to destroy teams. "There's no way to stop him," said Utah Jazz executive Scott Layden.

Hardaway was born September 1, 1966, in Chicago, Illinois, where his father, Donald, was a playground legend and inspired him to a life of hoops.

At the University of Texas-El Paso, Hardaway became the school's all-time scorer and was the 1989 Western Athletic Conference Player of the Year. He received the Naismith Basketball Hall of Fame Award as the nation's best collegian under 6 feet (he was 5'11" then).

Golden State selected him with the 14th pick in the 1989 NBA Draft and he made the All-NBA Rookie Team, the All-NBA Second Team in 1992, and the All-NBA Third Team in 1993.

He reached the 5,000-point, 2,500-assist plateau faster than any other player, except for Robertson, in NBA history, and he shares the record for most steals in a playoff game (8).

Year	Team	G	FG	FG Pct.	FT	FT Pct.	Reb.	Ast.	TP	Avg.
1989-90	Golden State	79	464	.471	211	.764	310	689	1162	14.7
1990-91	Golden State	82	739	.476	306	.803	332	793	1181	22.9
1991-92	Golden State	81	734	.461	298	.766	310	807	1893	23.4
1992-93	Golden State	66	522	.447	273	.744	263	699	1419	21.5
1993-94	Golden State				Injured					
	Totals	308	2459	.464	1088	.770	1215	2988	6355	20.6
Playoff Totals........................		13	122	.460	54	.720	48	130	325	25.0

The Ball Takes Odd Bounces

Some things are predictable. You know John Stockton is going to win the assists title and you could always count on Michael Jordan winning the scoring title. But it's the unexpected that adds even more spice to basketball.

Without a Guide Dog

Have you ever tried shooting with your eyes shut? Or blindfolded?

Ask Cedric Ceballos of the Lakers about how he does it. Or did it.

In 1992 in the NBA Slam-Dunk Championship at Florida's Orlando Arena, Cebellos wore a black blindfold on his last jump. He raced three-quarters of the length of the floor and slammed the ball home with both hands.

He'd already won the event when he tried the shot that capped a perfect score and brought him the $20,000 first prize.

"I call it the hocus-pocus," said Ceballos. "You count the steps. When running, it counts down to 10. I make it about 40 percent of the time.

"To all the kids out there: Don't try it at home."

Wilt's Sweetest Night

Hershey, Pennsylvania, is known the world over as the home of the chocolate bar. But to historians of pro basketball, Hershey means something else.

It was on March 2, 1962, that the Philadelphia Warriors met the New York Knicks in a regular-season NBA game at Hershey. This was considered a Philadelphia home game. The star of the Warriors was a 7'1" native of Philadelphia, Wilt Chamberlain. And this would be a night to remember.

Opening up with 23 points in the first quarter, Chamberlain had a total of 41 at the half and 69 before the third period had ended. In the fourth quarter, his teammates kept feeding him the ball in an effort to get Wilt past his own record of 78 points, which he had scored earlier in the season.

He not only broke the record, but he kept pouring the ball through the hoop. With less than a minute left, Wilt dunked a shot for his final 2 points. It gave him a total of 100 points for the night—a record that has never been matched.

He shot 36-for-63 from the field, 28-for-32 from the foul line. Oh, yes—the Warriors won, 169-147.

Free-Throw Fuss

Get the picture. Hall-of-Famer Calvin Murphy holds the NBA's season free-throw record of .958 (206-for-215).

Now we're in Houston for the last game of the 1993-94 season. The Rockets vs. the Denver Nuggets. Denver's Mahmoud Abdul-Rauf is fouled and gets two shots on the free-throw line. Murphy, retired as a Rocket since 1982 and sitting courtside, calls for the ball during a time-out.

Referee Derrick Stafford gives the ball to Murphy, who rubs it, then throws it back. Abdul-Rauf makes the first shot, but misses the second—and Murphy's record. Murphy applauds the miss as Abdul-Rauf finishes the season at .956.

It doesn't end there. There are complaints that Murphy put a "curse" on the ball and he shouldn't have been given it in the first place.

NBA Vice President Rod Thorn concluded that there was no harm in the referee's handoff. "It was during a time-out, not during play," Thorn said. "Abdul-Rauf didn't even see it. They talked before the game. They're good friends."

Case dismissed.

Caught in the Switch

Is it possible to play for two teams in the same NBA game?

The date was March 23, 1979, and the Philadelphia 76ers were hosting the New Jersey Nets in a game that had actually begun on November 8, 1978.

Philadelphia had seemingly won the November 8 game, 137-133, but Larry O'Brien, the NBA commissioner at the time, upheld the Nets' protest of a third technical foul called by referee Richie Powers on both Bernard King and Nets' coach Kevin Loughery. Under NBA rules, only two technical fouls could be called on any player or coach.

O'Brien ordered that the game be replayed from the point prior to the third technical foul called against King.

In the interim, however, four players had switched teams. On February 7, New Jersey traded Eric Money and Al Skinner to Philadelphia for Harvey Catchings, Ralph Simpson, and cash.

When the game resumed, with Philadelphia leading, 84-81, in the third quarter, the 76ers went on to win, 123-117.

None of the four players had much bearing on the outcome. Catchings fared the best, with 8 points and 4 rebounds for the Nets after having failed to score as a 76er in the original game. Simpson didn't score for the Nets after scoring 10 for Philadelphia, and Money had 4 points for Philadelphia after scoring 37 points for New Jersey in the first meeting.

"I remember looking at the box score the next day and seeing my name for both Philadelphia and New Jersey," said Catchings. "It was kind of weird, to say the least."

Indeed, in this one game it was possible to play for both teams.

(See box scores on next pages.)

ORIGINAL GAME

PHILADELPHIA 137, NEW JERSEY 133 (OT)

NEW JERSEY	FG	FT	Pts.	PHILADELPHIA	FG	FT	Pts.
King	3-11	2-2	8	Erving	9-25	6-8	24
Washington	7-14	4-6	18	B. Jones	4-6	2-2	10
Johnson	3-6	4-4	10	C. Jones	6-9	1-1	13
Money	15-26	7-12	37	Cheeks	1-7	0-0	2
Williamson	17-28	8-9	42	Collins	10-23	7-7	27
Elliott	0-1	0-0	0	Bibby	4-10	3-4	11
Boynes	1-4	0-0	2	Dawkins	8-10	1-2	17
V. Breda Kolff	5-7	0-0	10	Mix	6-17	5-6	17
Jordan	0-3	2-3	2	Simpson	5-7	0-2	10
Bassett	2-2	0-0	4	Bryant	3-7	0-0	6
Skinner	Did Not Play			Catchings	0-1	0-0	0
Totals	53-102	27-36	133	Totals	56-122	25-32	137

New Jersey...	38	32	27	22	8	6	—	133
Philadelphia ..	21	41	37	20	8	10	—	137

Rebounds: New Jersey 58 (Johnson 16), Philadelphia 55 (Erving 14); Assists: Philadelphia 42 (Bibby 10), New Jersey 26 (Money 9); Steals: Philadelphia 13 (Collins, Simpson 3), New Jersey 9 (Money 4); Blocked Shots: New Jersey 10 (Johnson 8), Philadelphia 6 (C. Jones, B. Jones 2); Officials: Richie Powers, Ed Middleton, Regan McCann; T: 2:30. A: 11,363.

REPLAYED GAME

PHILADELPHIA 123, NEW JERSEY 117

NEW JERSEY	FG	FT	PTS.	PHILADELPHIA	FG	FT	PTS.
King	3-11	2-2	8	Erving	11-25	10-13	32
Washington	5-7	2-2	12	B. Jones	8-11	3-4	19
Johnson	3-4	2-2	8	C. Jones	4-7	1-1	9
Money	11-16	1-2	23	Cheeks	1-6	0-0	2
Williamson	14-21	6-6	34	Collins	3-10	4-4	10
Elliott	0-1	0-0	0	Bibby	3-6	5-6	11
Boynes	1-3	0-0	2	Dawkins	6-6	1-2	13
V. Breda Kolff	5-8	2-4	12	Mix	3-9	3-4	9
Jordan	1-4	4-6	6	Simpson	4-6	0-0	8
Bassett	0-0	0-0	0	Bryant	3-7	0-0	6
Skinner	Did Not Play			Catchings	0-1	0-0	0
Catchings	2-4	4-4	8	Skinner	Did Not Play		
Simpson	0-0	0-0	0	Money	2-4	0-0	4
Jackson	2-7	0-0	4				
Totals	47-86	23-28	117	Totals	48-101	27-34	123

New Jersey	38	32	29	18	—	117
Philadelphia	21	41	34	27	—	123

Rebounds: Philadelphia 45 (B. Jones 9), New Jersey 44 (Johnson 10); Assists: Philadelphia 35 (Erving, Bibby 8), New Jersey 25 (Jordan 6); Steals: Philadelphia 10 (Collins, B. Jones 2), New Jersey 9 (Van Breda Kolff 3); Blocked Shots: New Jersey 13 (Johnson 8), Philadelphia 5 (Erving B., Jones 2); Officials: Earl Strom, Bill Saar, Jack Madden; T: 2:00. A: 11,368.

The Kid Who Shot Straight

Fourteen-year-old Craig (Clay) Schroeder fidgeted nervously as he approached the center-court stripe at Buffalo's Memorial Auditorium. This was at half-time of an NBA game in 1973 between the Buffalo Braves and the Los Angeles Lakers.

The players, returning to the court for warm-ups, paused interestedly as Clay, the 80th participant in the "Dodge Colt Shootout," said to himself, "Just get it close."

Clay leaned back and launched a left-handed push shot. It miraculously creased the cords, to the delight of 12,730 fans and one stunned 14-year-old.

He was too young to drive, but he had just won a Dodge Colt.

"As I walked away, Wilt Chamberlain said, 'I couldn't have made it' and Gail Goodrich and Jerry West told me 'Nice shot,'" Clay recalled.

The newspapers made a big thing of it, too. The *Tonawanda* (N.Y.) *News* knighted him with the nickname "Half-court." Another paper noted that he would be the first teenager whose father had to ask him for permission to use the car.

Clay was a freshman at Starpoint Central High School and he had no interest in pursuing a career in basketball. He was satisfied to have the best statistic of all—one-for-one from midcourt. Try and top that!

From Ballboy to TV Booth

He was nuts over basketball, and when he was a student at Abraham Lincoln High School in Brooklyn, New York, he formed a New York Knicks fan club. He started a newspaper, *Knick Knacks*, and the Knicks gave him a job as a ballboy. That's how it began for a boy named Marv Albert.

"In my spot behind the basket, I recovered shots and passes that went out of bounds. I was also errand boy, assistant trainer, and whatever else they needed me for," said Albert. "I was rubbing shoulders with NBA stars. This was the world I had always dreamed about, the world in which I wanted to be. For a kid . . . well, you can understand what all this meant."

The rest is broadcast history. Today, Albert is one of television's most celebrated sports announcers—No. 1 as the voice of the NBA's NBC telecasts.

Buckets by the Bushel

Colorado, famous for its mountain country, reached a new peak on December 13, 1983, when the Detroit Pistons defeated the Denver Nuggets, 186-184, in triple-overtime. It stands as the highest-scoring game in NBA history.

Guards Isiah Thomas, with 47 points, and John Long, 41, sparked the Pistons, and forwards Kiki Vandeweghe, with 51, and Alex English, 47, paced the Nuggets. The game was tied at 145 at the end of regulation time.

The 370-point total broke the record of 337 set by San Antonio (171) and Milwaukee (166) in 3 overtimes on March 6, 1982.

Lakers on a Roll

It all began on November 5, 1971, when the Los Angeles Lakers downed the Baltimore Bullets. Quarterbacked by Jerry West, with a cast that included Wilt Chamberlain, Jim McMillian, Gail Goodrich, and Happy Hairston, the Lakers were on a roll.

Home and away, the Lakers were a relentless machine, steamrolling opponent after opponent. They erased the NBA record of 20 straight victories set by the 1970-71 Milwaukee Bucks and just kept going. On December 22, the Lakers made it 27 straight victories, surpassing a 26-game streak by the New York Giants (baseball) to become the team with the longest winning streak in the history of organized pro sports.

The streak finally came to an end at 33 games on January 9, 1972, at the hands of the Bucks' Kareem Abdul-Jabbar and Oscar Robertson.

But the season continued on a high note as the Lakers recorded the best regular-season record (69-13) in NBA history and went on to win their first league title in Los Angeles.

TESTING...1...2...3

Here's something to do during a time-out—when you don't want to watch another commercial. And nobody's going to give you a bad mark if you don't know the answers.

Answers on pages 255-256.

Color Connection

Match the NBA team with its colors.

1. Charlotte Hornets
2. L.A. Lakers
3. Boston Celtics
4. Seattle SuperSonics
5. Orlando Magic
6. Indiana Pacers
7. Chicago Bulls
8. Golden St. Warriors
9. Phoenix Suns
10. San Antonio Spurs

a. Green & yellow
b. Blue & yellow
c. Gold & blue
d. Purple & orange
e. Purple & gold
f. Silver & black
g. Teal
h. Red & white
i. Green & white
j. Blue, silver & black

From Another Place

Match the team with its original NBA location.

1. L.A. Lakers		a.	Philadelphia
2. Detroit Pistons		b.	Buffalo
3. Utah Jazz		c.	Minneapolis
4. Golden St. Warriors		d.	New York
5. Washington Bullets		e.	Syracuse
6. New Jersey Nets		f.	San Diego
7. L.A. Clippers		g.	Rochester
8. Houston Rockets		h.	New Orleans
9. Sacramento Kings		i.	Chicago
10. Philadelphia		j.	Fort Wayne

Unscramble the Superstars

Juggle the letters until you come up with the names of current NBA players. If you have trouble, use the clues.

ailsqlehu eoaln _____
Clue: He's number 32 for the Orlando Magic.

drab gedutahyr _____
He's the man in the middle for the Cleveland Cavs.

aidvd oobnsnri _____
This Navy man was the NBA's scoring champ in 1993-94.

ihcmt hnorcmid _____
This Sacramento King started for the 1994 West All-Stars.

stioect ipnpep _____
He's won three championship rings with the Chicago Bulls.

tpciark geniw _____
He's the center of attention in New York's lineup.

hojn cstoontk _____
Need some assistance? He'll jazz up any offense.

snhwa dreylba _____
This player is 7'6" and a '76er.

gyumsg sbguoe _____
He's not tall, but is a big man in the Hornets' offense.

hrics uilmnl _____
He's scored big with Golden State and Dream Team I.

The Nickname Game

Match the player with his nickname.

 1. Wilt Chamberlain   a. The Admiral
 2. Earvin Johnson   b. The Dream
 3. Earl Monroe   c. Magic
 4. David Robinson   d. Tree
 5. Anferee Hardaway   e. Dr. J
 6. Michael Jordan   f. Clyde
 7. Walt Frazier   g. The Stilt
 8. Wayne Rollins   h. Air
 9. Hakeem Olajuwon   i. Penny
10. Julius Erving   j. The Pearl

Basketball Boggling

It's a scrambling game under the boards. Players fight for loose balls, bodies collide, fouls are called. Now find the common basketball terms that are scrambled in the puzzle below: DUNK, FOUL, GOAL, HOOK, JUMP, NET, RIM, SHOT.

Spell out each word, drawing a continuous line from one letter to another. You can go up, down, left, right, and on a slant—but you can't jump over any letter. Some letters will be used more than once.

R	Y	J	N	E
P	I	O	S	T
M	J	G	H	O
O	U	A	O	K
F	L	D	U	N

A-Maze-ing Search

Find the past or present NBA superstars in this wordsearch. The stars' last names will read right to left, left to right, vertically, horizontally, or diagonally.

```
C  A  P  R  I  R  G  N  I  W  E  S
R  H  D  A  F  O  R  O  D  M  A  N
E  G  A  N  A  D  R  O  J  K  N  O
B  N  E  M  W  M  E  C  I  R  P  W
B  I  R  O  B  I  N  S  O  N  E  I
E  N  E  L  A  E  N  O  A  S  N  L
W  R  L  A  M  A  R  R  T  B  O  K
P  U  L  B  I  F  N  L  G  U  L  I
W  O  I  Y  E  L  K  R  A  B  A  N
I  M  M  T  M  I  C  M  L  I  M  S
K  A  N  O  W  U  J  A  L  O  N  E
```

Barkley	Chamberlain	Ewing	Jordan	Malone
Miller	Mourning	Olajuwon	O'Neal	Price
Robinson	Rodman	Webber	West	Wilkins

YESTERDAY'S HEROES

■ ■ ■

Isiah Thomas is here. So are Larry Bird, Magic Johnson, and Kareem Abdul-Jabbar. It was only yesterday, or not much before, that they were making headlines. And now they're retired. But there is no forgetting these legendary players and their amazing achievements.

KAREEM ABDUL-JABBAR
Master of the Sky-Hook

The gambling town of Las Vegas, Nevada, seemed an unlikely setting for Kareem Abdul-Jabbar on April 5, 1984. The towering Laker center was there for a regular-season NBA game against the Utah Jazz.

In the fourth quarter, Kareem hit on his trademark sky- hook and the sellout crowd of more than 18,000 fans cheered wildly. The 7'2" veteran, in his 15th season, had broken Wilt Chamberlain's all-time NBA regular-season scoring record of 31,149 points.

Kareem would go on to play for five more record-making years before completing a unique and spectacular career at the age of 42. The picture of grace and elegance on the court, Kareem set a harvest of records and bagged awards galore, including six NBA championship rings.

Fantastic Facts About Kareem Abdul-Jabbar

(Born Ferdinand Lewis Alcindor)
Born: April 16, 1947, New York City, New York
Height: 7'2"
Weight: 267

•In his high school basketball career, Kareem led Power Memorial Academy to 71 straight victories. When Kareem played college ball at UCLA, the team had a record of 88-2 and won three NCAA titles.

•Kareem was the No. 1 draft pick in 1969. In his first season with the Milwaukee Bucks he was the NBA's second-leading scorer and was named Rookie of the Year.

•Kareem is the NBA's all-time leading scorer with 38,387 points. He's also No. 1 in field goals made, field goals attempted, blocked shots, most games played, and most personal fouls.

•He was named NBA MVP 6 times, All-NBA First Team 10 times, NBA All-Defensive Team 5 times, and NBA Finals MVP twice.

Year	Team	G	FG	FG Pct.	FT	FT Pct.	Reb.	Ast.	TP	Avg.
1969-70	Milwaukee	82	938	.518	485	.653	1190	337	2361	28.8
1970-71	Milwaukee	82	1063	.577	470	.690	1311	272	2596	31.7
1971-72	Milwaukee	81	1159	.574	504	.689	1346	370	2822	34.8
1972-73	Milwaukee	76	982	.554	328	.713	1224	379	2292	30.2
1973-74	Milwaukee	81	948	.539	295	.702	1178	386	2191	27.0
1974-75	Milwaukee	65	812	.513	325	.763	912	264	1949	30.0
1975-76	Los Angeles ...	82	914	.529	447	.703	1383	413	2275	27.7
1976-77	Los Angeles ...	82	888	.579	376	.701	1090	319	2152	26.2
1977-78	Los Angeles ...	62	663	.550	274	.783	801	269	1600	25.8
1978-79	Los Angeles ...	80	777	.577	349	.736	1025	431	1903	23.8
1979-80	Los Angeles ...	82	835	.604	364	.765	886	371	2034	24.8
1980-81	Los Angeles ...	80	836	.574	423	.766	821	272	2095	26.2
1981-82	Los Angeles ...	76	753	.579	312	.706	659	225	1818	23.9
1982-83	Los Angeles ...	79	722	.588	278	.749	592	200	1722	21.8
1983-84	Los Angeles ...	80	716	.578	285	.723	587	211	1717	21.5
1984-85	L.A. Lakers	79	723	.599	289	.732	622	249	1735	22.0
1985-86	L.A. Lakers	79	755	.564	336	.765	478	280	1846	23.4
1986-87	L.A. Lakers	78	560	.564	245	.714	523	203	1366	17.5
1987-88	L.A. Lakers	80	480	.532	205	.762	478	135	1165	14.6
1988-89	L.A. Lakers	74	313	.475	122	.739	334	74	748	10.1
	Totals..............	1560	15837	.559	6712	.721	17440	5660	38387	24.6
Playoff Totals..................		237	2356	.533	1050	.740	2481	767	5762	24.3

LARRY BIRD
An All-Around Superstar

As a boy growing up in tiny French Lick, Indiana, Larry Bird didn't own a bike. His mother couldn't afford one. But he and his brothers had a basketball. And almost every day, Larry dribbled the ball up and down the hilly streets to the local playground, where he played from sunrise to sunset.

Nothing else mattered to him, but mastery of the game he loved. When he was in high school, his coach "banged the fundamentals" into him over and over. Hour after hour, Bird designed his moves and worked to strengthen his left hand. "I never wanted to leave the court until I got things exactly correct," he said. "My dream was to become a pro."

Larry Bird's dream came true in 1978 when he was selected by the Boston Celtics in the NBA Draft. Almost from the start of his pro career, he became the most complete basketball player to come into the league since Oscar Robertson. He could score, pass, play defense, and lead a team. In 13 seasons, Bird took the Celtics to three NBA championships and, along with Magic Johnson, changed the concept of the game with leadership, unselfishness, competitive spirit, and flair for the dramatic.

Fantastic Facts About Larry Bird

Born: December 7, 1956, West Baden, Illinois
Height: 6'9"
Weight: 220

•Larry led Indiana State to the NCAA championship game in 1979, losing to Magic Johnson-led Michigan State. Bird was named College Player of the Year that year.

•The year before the Celtics got Bird they were 29-53, last in the Atlantic Division. In his first year, 1979-80, he led Boston to the NBA's best record, 61-29, and was named Rookie of the Year.

•Bird was named the NBA's MVP in 1984, 1985, and 1986, and he was All-NBA First Team 9 straight years, from 1980 to 1988.

•According to Celtics coach, Red Auerbach, Larry was "the best passing big man" he'd ever seen. Bird handed out more assists (5,695) than any other forward in the history of the game.

•Larry Bird was a member of the Dream Team that won a gold medal at the 1992 Barcelona Olympics.

Year	Team	G	FG	FG Pct.	FT	FT Pct.	Reb.	Ast.	TP	Avg.
1979-80	Boston	82	693	.474	301	.836	852	370	1745	21.3
1980-81	Boston	82	719	.478	283	.863	895	451	1741	21.2
1981-82	Boston	77	711	.503	328	.863	837	447	1761	22.9
1982-83	Boston	79	747	.504	351	.840	870	458	1867	23.6
1983-84	Boston	79	758	.492	374	.888	796	520	1908	24.2
1984-85	Boston	80	918	.522	403	.882	842	531	2295	28.7
1985-86	Boston	82	796	.496	441	.896	805	557	2115	25.8
1986-87	Boston	74	786	.525	414	.910	682	566	2076	28.1
1987-88	Boston	76	881	.527	415	.916	703	467	2275	29.9
1988-89	Boston	6	49	.471	18	.947	37	29	116	19.3
1989-90	Boston	75	718	.473	319	.930	712	562	1820	24.3
1990-91	Boston	60	462	.454	163	.891	509	431	1164	19.4
1991-92	Boston	45	353	.466	150	.926	434	306	908	20.2
Totals		897	8591	.496	3960	.886	8974	5695	21791	24.3
Playoff Totals		164	1458	.472	901	.890	1683	1062	3897	23.8

WILT CHAMBERLAIN
"The Big Dipper"

When Wilt Chamberlain was a high school senior in Philadelphia in 1955, an article entitled "The High School Kid Who Could Play Pro Right Now" appeared in *Sport* magazine. Wilt was already a 7-footer and everyone agreed that it was only a matter of time before he would become a towering force in the game.

Four years later everyone found out just what kind of impact Wilt would have on pro basketball. In 1959-60, his first season with the Philadelphia 76ers, "Wilt the Stilt" (later "The Big Dipper") led the NBA in scoring with an awesome 37.6 point average and was named Rookie of the Year.

For the first seven years of his career, Wilt's teams never won a championship. His critics said Wilt selfishly scored points and ignored other aspects of his game that might help his team win. But in 1966-67, Wilt changed his style. He concentrated less on shooting and more on passing. He blocked rivals' shots and went for every rebound. Result: He led the 76ers to the NBA title and was named regular-season MVP. Wilt won a second championship ring with the Los Angeles Lakers in 1972. He retired after the next season, but Wilt left his mark on both the game and the record book.

Fantastic Facts About Wilt Chamberlain

Born: August 21, 1936, Philadelphia, Pennsylvania
Height: 7'1"
Weight: 275

•Wilt once grabbed a record 55 rebounds in a game against the Boston Celtics in 1960. He led the NBA in rebounding 11 seasons.

•Wilt is the only player to ever score over 4,000 points in a season. A four-time NBA MVP, he led the NBA in scoring seven straight seasons from 1960 to 1966.

•Wilt holds the single-game record for most points, 100, most field goals attempted, 63, and most field goals made, 36. He also scored the most points in an All-Star Game, 42. Although Wilt was a 50 percent foul shooter, he still holds the record for most free throws made in a game, 28.

•Wilt never fouled out in 1,205 regular season and playoff games.

•Wilt made a record 18 consecutive field goals in a 1963 game against the Knicks.

Year	Team	G	FG	FG Pct.	FT	FT Pct.	Reb.	Ast.	TP	Avg.
1959-60	Philadelphia ...	72	1065	.461	577	.582	1941	168	2707	37.6
1960-61	Philadelphia ...	79	1251	.509	531	.504	2149	148	3033	38.4
1961-62	Philadelphia ...	80	1597	.506	835	.613	2052	192	4029	50.4
1962-63	San Francisco.	80	1463	.528	660	.593	1946	275	3586	44.8
1963-64	San Francisco.	80	1204	.524	540	.531	1787	403	2948	36.9
1964-65	S.F.-Phil.	73	1063	.510	408	.464	1673	250	2534	34.7
1965-66	Philadelphia ...	79	1074	.540	501	.513	1943	414	2649	33.5
1966-67	Philadelphia ...	81	785	.683	386	.441	1957	630	1956	24.1
1967-68	Philadelphia ...	82	819	.595	354	.380	1952	702	1992	24.3
1968-69	Los Angeles ...	81	641	.583	382	.446	1712	366	1664	20.5
1969-70	Los Angeles ...	12	129	.568	70	.446	221	49	328	27.3
1970-71	Los Angeles ...	82	668	.545	360	.538	1493	352	1696	20.7
1971-72	Los Angeles ...	82	496	.649	221	.422	1572	329	1213	14.8
1972-73	Los Angeles ...	82	426	.727	232	.510	1526	365	1084	13.2
Totals..............		1045	12681	.540	6057	.511	23924	4643	31419	30.1
Playoff Totals..................		160	1425	.522	757	.465	3913	673	3607	22.5

BOB COUSY
Court Magician

Houdini is considered the most famous magician of all time. In basketball, there was no magician to compare with the Boston Celtics' Bob Cousy. He was a ball-handling wizard whose behind-the-back passes and dazzling playmaking inspired sportswriters to label him "Houdini of the Hardwood."

"The Cooz," as he later became known, learned the game on the playgrounds of St. Albans, Queens, a borough of New York City. Later he led Holy Cross to the 1947 NCAA crown. He would go on to play a major role, with Bill Russell, in six Celtics championships. He was such a valuable member of the Celtics squad that when he retired, Boston coach Red Auerbach said, "What can you say when you know you're going to lose the greatest backcourt man who ever lived?"

Fantastic Facts About Bob Cousy

Born: August 9, 1928, New York City, New York
Height: 6'1"
Weight: 175

•Cousy was the NBA MVP in 1957 and was named to the All-NBA First Team 10 straight years, from 1952 to 1961.

•Cousy played in 13 straight All-Star Games.

•Beginning in 1952-53, Cousy led the NBA in assists eight consecutive years.

•Cousy set a record for most assists in one half in 1959 with 17 against Minneapolis.

•Cousy played seven games for the Cincinnati Royals when he coached the team in 1969-70. He was the oldest performer to play in the league at that time.

Year	Team	G	FG	FG Pct.	FT	FT Pct.	Reb.	Ast.	TP	Avg.
1950-51	Boston	69	401	.352	276	.756	474	341	1078	15.6
1951-52	Boston	66	512	.369	409	.808	421	441	1433	21.7
1952-53	Boston	71	464	.352	479	.816	449	547	1407	19.8
1953-54	Boston	72	486	.385	411	.787	394	518	1383	19.2
1954-55	Boston	71	522	.397	460	.807	424	557	1504	21.2
1955-56	Boston	72	440	.360	476	.844	492	642	1356	18.8
1956-57	Boston	64	478	.378	363	.821	309	478	1319	20.6
1957-58	Boston	65	445	.353	277	.850	322	463	1167	18.0
1958-59	Boston	65	484	.384	329	.855	359	557	1297	20.0
1959-60	Boston	75	568	.384	319	.792	352	715	1455	19.4
1960-61	Boston	76	513	.371	352	.779	331	591	1378	18.1
1961-62	Boston	75	462	.391	251	.754	261	584	1175	15.7
1962-63	Boston	76	392	.397	219	.735	201	515	1003	13.2
1969-70	Cincinnati	7	1	.333	3	1.000	5	10	5	0.7
	Totals..............	924	6168	.375	4624	.803	4794	6959	16960	18.4
	Playoff Totals..................	109	689	.342	640	.801	546	937	2018	18.5

JULIUS ERVING
"Dr. J"

He was a superstar, but he seemed superhuman. He stood 6'6", 220 pounds, but his shoulders and arms bordered on massive. His legs were sleek and powerful, his hands positively enormous. But what really set Julius Winfield Erving, Jr. apart from all other basketball players in the 1970s were his above-the-hoop flights and show-stopping moves. He created new standards for excellence and excitement in pro basketball. Erving captivated fans by doing things that had never been seen before. His twirling dunks and acrobatic moves became the stuff of legend.

As a high school basketball star Erving was fearless and flamboyant, trying to do trickery with the ball while scoring at the same time. When he got the nickname "Dr. J," many thought it was because of his precise and delicate moves. But Erving said it really derived from a friend after Julius told him he was going to be a doctor.

He began his pro career in 1971 with the Virginia Squires in the ABA (American Basketball Association). Virginia sold him to the New Jersey Nets in 1973 and he promptly led them to the ABA title. Later, after the ABA merged with the NBA, he joined the Philadelphia 76ers and became a Philadelphia folk hero—for his on-court exploits and his grace and eloquence off-court. Today, Dr. J remains an ambassador for the game of basketball and a hero to many of today's NBA stars.

Fantastic Facts About Julius Erving

Born: February 22, 1950, Roosevelt, New York
Height: 6'6"
Weight: 220

•Erving not only led the Nets to two ABA titles, he also led the 76ers to the NBA title in 1983.

•Dr. J was a 3-time ABA MVP and a 1-time NBA MVP.

•In both 1977 and 1983 Erving was the All-Star Game MVP.

•During his college career, Erving became one of a select group of players to average 20 points and 20 rebounds per game.

•In his combined ABA-NBA career, Erving scored more than 30,000 points.

Year	Team	G	FG	FG Pct.	FT	FT Pct.	Reb.	Ast.	TP	Avg.
1971-72	Virginia (ABA) ..	84	910	.498	467	.745	1319	335	2290	27.3
1972-73	Virginia (ABA) ..	71	894	.496	475	.776	867	298	2268	31.9
1973-74	New York (ABA)	84	914	.512	454	.766	899	434	2299	27.4
1974-75	New York (ABA)	84	914	.506	486	.799	914	462	2343	27.9
1975-76	New York (ABA)	84	949	.507	530	.801	925	423	2462	29.3
1976-77	Philadelphia ...	82	685	.499	400	.777	695	306	1770	21.6
1977-78	Philadelphia ...	74	611	.502	306	.845	481	279	1528	20.6
1978-79	Philadelphia ...	78	715	.491	373	.745	564	357	1803	23.1
1979-80	Philadelphia ...	78	838	.519	420	.787	576	355	2100	26.9
1980-81	Philadelphia ...	82	794	.521	422	.787	657	364	2014	24.6
1981-82	Philadelphia ...	81	780	.546	411	.763	557	319	1974	24.4
1982-83	Philadelphia ...	72	605	.517	330	.759	491	263	1542	21.4
1983-84	Philadelphia ...	77	678	.512	364	.754	532	309	1727	22.4
1984-85	Philadelphia ...	78	610	.494	338	.765	414	233	1561	20.0
1985-86	Philadelphia ...	74	521	.480	289	.785	370	248	1340	18.1
1986-87	Philadelphia ...	60	400	.471	191	.813	264	191	1005	16.8
	NBA Totals......	836	7237	.507	3844	.777	5601	3224	18364	22.0
	ABA Totals......	407	4581	.504	2412	.778	4924	1952	11662	28.7
	NBA Playoff Totals..........	141	1187	.486	707	.779	994	594	3088	21.9
	ABA Playoff Totals..........	48	582	.519	318	.795	617	247	1492	31.1

MAGIC JOHNSON
"Showtime"

When he was at Everett High School in Lansing, Michigan, a local sportswriter called him "Magic." Magic because of his effervescent smile. Magic because he was such a talented basketball player. But mostly he was Magic be-cause he somehow transformed good teams into great teams. Earvin Johnson did that everywhere he went—in high school, at Michigan State, and then with the Los Angeles Lakers.

The No. 1 pick overall in the 1979 Draft, Magic turned on the Lakers and the league immediately with his joyful exuberance. Magic quickly introduced "Showtime" and "Winnin' Time" to the Hollywood crowd. And fittingly, the ending to his remarkable rookie year was pure Hollywood. After leading the Lakers through the playoffs, Magic started at center in place of the injured Abdul-Jabbar in the decisive Game 6 of the 1980 NBA Finals against Philadelphia. He finished with 42 points, 15 rebounds, and 7 assists in one of the greatest playoff efforts of all time, giving the Lakers the NBA crown. He was the Finals MVP and named to the All-Rookie team.

With Magic at the point—"a coach on the floor," his former coach Pat Riley called him—the Lakers won five championships in the 1980s.

Magic retired in 1992 after announcing that he had contracted the virus that causes AIDS. In 1994, he coached the Lakers for a stint, before becoming part-owner of the team he served so magically on the court.

Fantastic Facts About Magic Johnson

Born: August 14, 1959, Lansing, Michigan
Height: 6'9"
Weight: 220

•In 1977 Magic led his Everett High School team to a 27-1 record and the state championship. Two years later, he helped Michigan State win the NCAA title.

•Magic was the NBA's regular season MVP three times, Playoff MVP three times, and All-Star Game MVP once.

•Magic was named to the All-NBA First Team nine times.

•As a member of the 1992 Dream Team, Magic won a gold medal at the Barcelona Olympics.

•Magic and Larry Bird engaged in legendary duels throughout their NBA careers. In Bird's opinion, "Magic is the best basketball player I've ever seen."

•As of the beginning of the 1994-95 season, Magic was the NBA's all-time assist leader.

Year	Team	G	FG	FG Pct.	FT	FT Pct.	Reb.	Ast.	TP	Avg.
1979-80	Los Angeles ...77		503	.530	374	.810	596	563	1387	18.0
1980-81	Los Angeles ...37		312	.532	171	.760	320	317	798	21.6
1981-82	Los Angeles ...78		556	.537	329	.760	751	743	1447	18.6
1982-83	Los Angeles ...79		511	.548	304	.800	683	829	1326	16.8
1983-84	Los Angeles ...67		441	.565	290	.810	491	875	1178	17.6
1984-85	Los Angeles ...77		504	.561	391	.843	476	968	1406	18.3
1985-86	Los Angeles ...72		483	.526	378	.871	426	907	1354	18.8
1986-87	Los Angeles ...80		683	.522	535	.848	504	977	1909	23.9
1987-88	Los Angeles ...72		490	.492	417	.853	449	858	1408	19.6
1988-89	Los Angeles ...77		579	.509	513	.911	607	988	1730	22.5
1989-90	Los Angeles ...79		546	.480	567	.890	522	907	1765	22.3
1990-91	Los Angeles ...79		466	.477	519	.906	551	989	1531	19.4
	Totals	874	6074	.521	4788	.848	6376	9921	17239	19.7
Playoff Totals		186	1276	.508	1040	.838	1431	2320	3640	19.6

OSCAR ROBERTSON
"The Big O"

For youngsters and oldsters alike, Oscar Robertson held a clinic in basketball technique every time he stepped onto the court. All you needed was a ticket to the game. Then you watched his every move.

No guard shot better. No guard rebounded better. No guard excelled so consistently as the player known as "The Big O." In a marvelous 14-year NBA career, Robertson set new standards for guard play.

A scoring star in both high school and college, Robertson was a key member of the 1960 U.S. Olympic team that won a gold medal in Rome. That same year he joined the Cincinnati Royals. He had played forward exclusively as a collegian, but switched to guard as a pro and was Rookie of the Year in 1961, averaging 30.5 points and 9.7 assists, setting a playmaking record he would exceed many times.

Despite Robertson's enormous presence over a 10-year period, the Royals never won a championship. But Robertson did, after being traded to the Milwaukee Bucks in 1970. Robertson was 32 by then and the Bucks were being built around a young center named Kareem Abdul-Jabbar. Robertson gave the Bucks just the sort of leadership and inspiration they needed. And they won the title in 1970-71.

Fantastic Facts About Oscar Robertson

Born: November 24, 1938, Charlotte, Tennessee
Height: 6'5"
Weight: 205

•Robertson led his high school team to 45 straight victories and two straight state championships. At the University of Cincinnati, Robertson led the nation in scoring and was College Player of the Year three seasons.

•In 1961-62, his second season, Robertson achieved something no other player has done by averaging a triple-double for the entire season—30.8 points, 12.5 rebounds, and 11.4 assists per game.

•The Big O was named to the All-NBA First Team nine times.

•He was the NBA MVP in 1964 and All-Star game MVP three times.

•Robertson led the NBA in assists six times.

Year	Team	G	FG	FG Pct.	FT	FT Pct.	Reb.	Ast.	TP	Avg.
1960-61	Cincinnati	71	756	.473	653	.822	716	690	2165	30.5
1961-62	Cincinnati	79	866	.478	700	.803	985	899	2432	30.8
1962-63	Cincinnati	80	825	.518	614	.810	835	758	2264	28.3
1963-64	Cincinnati	79	840	.483	800	.853	783	868	2480	31.4
1964-65	Cincinnati	75	807	.480	665	.839	674	861	2279	30.4
1965-66	Cincinnati	76	818	.475	742	.842	586	847	2378	31.3
1966-67	Cincinnati	79	838	.493	736	.873	486	845	2412	30.5
1967-68	Cincinnati	65	660	.500	576	.873	391	633	1896	29.2
1968-69	Cincinnati	79	656	.486	643	.838	502	772	1955	24.7
1969-70	Cincinnati	69	647	.511	454	.809	422	558	1748	25.3
1970-71	Milwaukee	81	592	.496	385	.850	462	668	1569	19.4
1971-72	Milwaukee	64	419	.472	276	.836	323	491	1114	17.4
1972-73	Milwaukee	73	446	.454	238	.847	360	551	1130	15.5
1973-74	Milwaukee	70	338	.438	212	.835	279	446	888	12.7
Totals		1040	9508	.485	7694	.838	7804	9887	26710	25.7
Playoff Totals		86	675	.460	560	.855	578	769	1910	22.2

BILL RUSSELL
Dean of Defense

From 1957 to 1969 the Boston Celtics were a dynasty that won 11 NBA titles, 8 of them in a row. One of the biggest reasons for the Celtics' success was their sensational center Bill Russell.

Selected third overall by the Boston Celtics in the 1956 NBA Draft, he introduced rebounding and shot-blocking as new art forms in the pro game. Russell's awesome cat-like movements and tremendous timing intimidated countless shooters. His mobility helped redefine the center position. His unique skills made him the greatest defensive player in NBA history.

"He was the ultimate team player," Hall-of-Fame Celtic Bob Cousy said. "Without Bill there would have been no Celtic dynasty."

Or fabled Celtic fast break. It was Russell's mastery of the boards that got the ball in the hands of his fast-breaking teammates. He developed a sound hook shot and good baseline shot, and he glorified the blocked shot.

In 1967, he became Boston's player-coach, the first black coach in NBA history. After conquering every challenge, the fiercely-proud Hall-of-Famer retired at the age of 35.

Fantastic Facts About Bill Russell

Born: February 12, 1934, Monroe, Louisiana
Height: 6'10"
Weight: 220

Charles Barkley

Karl Malone and David Robinson

Michael Jordan

Chris Mullin, Shawn Bradley, and Latrell Sprewell

Alonzo Mourning

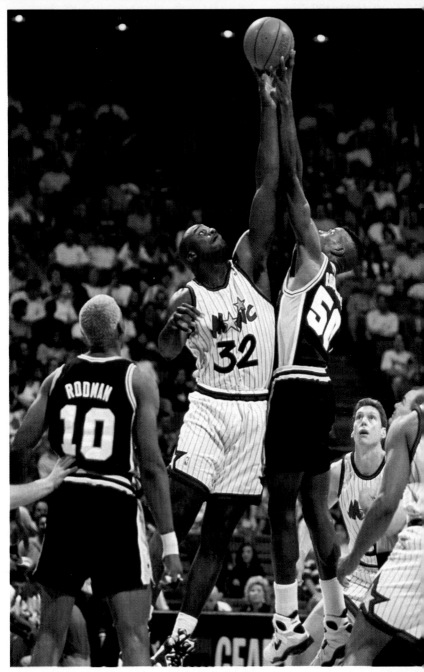

Shaquille O'Neal

Muggsy Bogues

Gary Payton

- Russell was the NBA MVP five times and an All-NBA First Team selection three times.

- In a 1957 game against Philadelphia, Russell grabbed 32 rebounds in one half, setting an NBA record. He led the NBA in rebounding four seasons, and in his 13-year career averaged an amazing 22.5 rebounds per game.

- He won a gold medal at the 1956 Olympic Games in Melbourne, Australia.

- He was named to the NBA 25th and 35th Anniversary All-Time Teams in 1970 and 1980.

- Russell was selected as "the Greatest Player in the History of the NBA" by the Professional Basketball Writers Association of America in 1980.

Year	Team	G	FG	FG Pct.	FT	FT Pct.	Reb.	Ast.	TP	Avg.
1956-57	Boston	48	277	.427	152	.492	943	88	706	14.7
1957-58	Boston	69	456	.442	230	.519	1564	202	1142	16.6
1958-59	Boston	70	456	.457	256	.598	1612	222	1168	16.7
1959-60	Boston	74	555	.467	240	.612	1778	277	1350	18.2
1960-61	Boston	78	532	.426	258	.550	1868	264	1322	16.9
1961-62	Boston	76	575	.457	286	.595	1891	341	1436	18.9
1962-63	Boston	78	511	.432	287	.555	1843	348	1309	16.8
1963-64	Boston	78	466	.433	236	.550	1930	370	1168	15.0
1964-65	Boston	78	429	.438	244	.573	1878	410	1102	14.1
1965-66	Boston	78	391	.415	223	.551	1779	371	1005	12.9
1966-67	Boston	81	395	.454	285	.610	1700	472	1075	13.3
1967-68	Boston	78	365	.425	247	.537	1451	357	977	12.5
1968-69	Boston	77	279	.433	204	.526	1484	374	762	9.9
Totals		963	5687	.440	3148	.561	21721	4096	14522	15.1
Playoff Totals		165	1003	.430	667	.603	4104	770	2673	16.2

ISIAH THOMAS
Zig-Zagging with "Zeke"

He was the youngest of Mary Thomas' nine children, growing up in a Chicago ghetto surrounded by drugs and street gangs. But Isiah Lord Thomas managed to avoid getting caught in the net of that troubled world. Instead, he found escape in basketball.

And basketball never saw a more dominant "little man" than Isiah Thomas. A free-spirited point guard with an engaging smile, Thomas was a dazzling passer, fearless penetrator, and one of the game's great clutch shooters, as well as a born leader.

The Detroit Pistons chose him No. 2 out of Indiana in the 1981 draft. He became the team leader on and off the court, bringing together a mix of personalities known as the "Bad Boys" for their aggressive play. Thomas ultimately took the team to back-to-back titles in 1989 and 1990.

He was equally deft with the 3-point shot as he was scoring in traffic, often outmaneuvering 7-footers. Thomas was respected as one of a handful of players in the 1980s—along with Larry Bird, Michael Jordan, and Magic Johnson—who could almost single-handedly take over a game.

"He had a lot of heart," said former teammate Vinnie Johnson. "Whatever the team needed, 'Zeke' provided it. He showed that with sacrifice, you could win."

Fantastic Facts About Isiah Thomas

Born: April 30, 1961, Chicago, Illinois
Height: 6'1"
Weight: 185

•Thomas is the Detroit Pistons' team leader in points, assists, and steals. He led the NBA in assists in 1985.

•Thomas was the MVP in the NBA Finals in 1990 and All-Star Game MVP twice.

•He was named to the All-NBA First Team three times.

•In a playoff game against Los Angeles in 1988, Thomas set an NBA record by scoring 25 points in a quarter.

•He was a member of the 1980 U.S. Olympic Team.

Year	Team	G	FG	FG Pct.	FT	FT Pct.	Reb.	Ast.	TP	Avg.
1981-82	Detroit...........	72	453	.424	302	.704	209	565	1225	17.0
1982-83	Detroit...........	81	725	.472	368	.710	328	634	1854	22.9
1983-84	Detroit...........	82	669	.462	388	.733	327	914	1748	21.3
1984-85	Detroit...........	81	646	.458	399	.809	361	1123	1720	21.2
1985-86	Detroit...........	77	609	.488	365	.790	277	830	1609	20.9
1986-87	Detroit...........	81	626	.463	400	.768	319	813	1671	20.6
1987-88	Detroit...........	81	621	.463	305	.774	278	678	1577	19.5
1988-89	Detroit...........	80	569	.464	287	.818	273	663	1458	18.2
1989-90	Detroit...........	81	579	.438	292	.775	308	765	1492	18.4
1990-91	Detroit...........	48	289	.435	179	.782	160	446	776	16.2
1991-92	Detroit...........	78	564	.446	292	.772	247	560	1445	18.5
1992-93	Detroit...........	79	526	.418	278	.737	232	671	1391	17.6
1993-94	Detroit...........	58	318	.417	181	.702	159	399	856	14.8
	Totals.............	979	7194	.452	4036	.759	3478	9061	18822	19.2
Playoff Totals..................		111	825	.441	530	.769	524	987	2261	20.4

JERRY WEST
"Mr. Clutch"

Like most great players, Jerry West was superb under pressure. "I learned," he once said, "that no matter what happens in a game, the last four minutes seem to decide it. So when it comes, I'm ready."

So ready was he on so many occasions that he earned the nickname "Mr. Clutch." Nobody could deny that description, for he won countless regular-season games, playoff games, and the 1972 All-Star Game with clutch shots.

In the 1969 NBA Finals, West's Los Angeles Lakers were battling the Boston Celtics for the sixth time in eight seasons. The previous five series had ended in defeat for Los Angeles. And now it came down to Game 7. But the Celtics won again, despite West's 42 points, 13 rebounds, and 12 assists.

Celtic captain John Havlicek put his arm around Jerry and told him how much the team respected him and how they hoped one day he would win a championship. He and the Lakers finally did—in a 1971-72 season in which Los Angeles had an incredible 33-game winning streak.

Fantastic Facts About Jerry West

Born: May 28, 1938, Cheylan, West Virginia
Height: 6'3"
Weight: 175

•When West retired after the 1973-74 season he was the third-leading scorer in NBA history with 25,192 points. He had averaged 27 points per game. In a remarkable game against the Knicks, West poured in 63 points.

•West was a member of the U.S. Olympic team that won the gold medal in Rome in 1960.

•He was an All-NBA First Team selection 10 times and NBA All-Defensive First Team four straight seasons (1970-73)

•Mr. Clutch was the Playoff MVP in 1969 and All-Star Game MVP in 1972.

•In 1965-66 West made 840 free throws, setting an NBA one-season record.

Year	Team	G	FG	FG Pct.	FT	FT Pct.	Reb.	Ast.	TP	Avg.
1960-61	Los Angeles ...	79	529	.419	331	.666	611	333	1389	17.6
1961-62	Los Angeles ...	75	799	.445	712	.769	591	402	2310	30.8
1962-63	Los Angeles ...	55	559	.461	371	.778	384	307	1489	27.1
1963-64	Los Angeles ...	72	740	.484	584	.832	443	403	2064	28.7
1964-65	Los Angeles ...	74	822	.497	648	.821	447	364	2292	31.0
1965-66	Los Angeles ...	79	818	.473	840	.860	562	480	2476	31.3
1966-67	Los Angeles ...	66	645	.464	602	.878	392	447	1892	28.7
1967-68	Los Angeles ...	51	476	.514	391	.811	294	310	1343	26.3
1968-69	Los Angeles ...	61	545	.471	490	.821	262	423	1580	25.9
1969-70	Los Angeles ...	74	831	.497	647	.824	338	554	2309	31.2
1970-71	Los Angeles ...	69	667	.494	525	.832	320	655	1859	26.9
1971-72	Los Angeles ...	77	735	.477	515	.814	327	747	1985	25.8
1972-73	Los Angeles ...	69	618	.479	339	.805	289	607	1575	22.8
1973-74	Los Angeles ...	31	232	.447	165	.833	116	206	629	20.3
Totals..............		932	9016	.474	7160	.814	5376	6238	25192	27.0
Playoff Totals..................		153	1622	.469	1213	.805	855	970	4457	29.1

A BARREL OF HOOPS

▬ ▬ ▬

Basketball/Baseball Pros

At the rate Michael Jordan was going as a minor-league baseball player in the summer of 1994, it was still too early to tell whether he would join a rare group—athletes who have played in the majors in basketball and baseball.

They range from the late Chuck Connors, best known as the star of *The Rifleman* TV series, to the NBA's Danny Ainge.

Here are the two-way guys:

Chuck Connors—He played with the Rochester Royals and Boston Celtics from 1945-48 and, as a first baseman, had one at-bat with the Brooklyn Dodgers in 1949 and 66 games with the Chicago Cubs in 1951.

Danny Ainge—Before starting an NBA career that began with Boston and has taken him to Sacramento, Portland, and Phoenix, Ainge was a major-league infielder/outfielder with the Toronto Blue Jays.

Dick Groat—An All-American basketball player at Duke, Groat played in the NBA in 1952-53 with the Fort Wayne Pistons. Then he turned to baseball as a shortstop for 14 years with the Pirates, Cardinals, and Phillies.

Gene Conley—As a center and a pitcher, Conley

actually mixed basketball and baseball, often playing both sports in the same years, starting in 1952. He was a Celtic and a Knick, and played for the Boston and Milwaukee Braves, the Phillies, and Red Sox.

Dave DeBusschere—Two short seasons (3 wins, 4 losses) as a White Sox pitcher inspired DeBusschere to be a full-time hoopster. Starting in 1962, this 6'6", 220-pound master of defense had a 12-year NBA career with the Pistons and Knicks. DeBusschere was a member of New York's championship teams in 1970 and 1973.

Ron Reed—The Notre Dame alumnus tried basketball with the Pistons for two years (1965-67) and went on to a 19-year baseball career as a pitcher with the Braves, Phillies, and White Sox. He was a member of the World Series-winning Phillies in 1980.

Charles (Cotton) Nash—The 6'8" Nash was a Kentucky All-American who played for the Los Angeles Lakers and San Francisco Warriors in 1964-65, and had an equally short-lived career as a first baseman with the White Sox (1967) and Twins (1969,1970). But, no matter the number of games, he can say he played in the majors in baseball and basketball.

"Blaze's" All-Time Women's Top 10

Growing up in Cranford, New Jersey, Carol Blazejowski played one-on-one and three-on-three with the boys. "I wasn't as strong, not as tall, and couldn't jump as high," she said. "But none of them could shoot as well."

How she could shoot! Carol first made newspaper headlines with the nickname "Blaze" when she led Cranford High School to the state final in her senior year.

In the changing era of women's basketball, when the old 6-player half-court game went to 5-player full-court, she became the most dominant player in the sport at Montclair State. The 5'11", eagle-eyed guard scored 52 points in a game at Madison Square Garden, became the national all-time scoring leader, and won the Wade Trophy as Women's Basketball Player of the Year in 1978.

And she was selected for the 1980 Olympic team that never got to Moscow because the United States withdrew from the Games.

The NBA didn't draft her, but "Blaze" played in the newly formed Women's Basketball League in 1980-81. It only lasted a year, but she was MVP and won the scoring title.

"Blaze" did make it to the NBA. Today she's a director of licensing for NBA Properties.

Carol was asked to name her all-time women's team. She had to be included, she was told. No problem. You'll see "Blaze," who was elected to the Hall of Fame in 1994, on the top of the list that follows.

1. Carol "Blaze" Blazejowski, Montclair State
2. Anne Meyers, UCLA
3. Nancy Lieberman, Old Dominion
4. Cheryl Miller, USC
5. Lynette Woodard, Kansas
6. Lusia Harris, Delta State
7. Theresa Edwards, Georgia
8. Clarissa Davis, Texas
9. Theresa Shank, Immaculata
10. Bridget Gordon, Tennessee

A Rookie's Goof

Derek Harper was especially pleased to be in the NBA playoffs. He was a rookie guard out of the University of Illinois, playing for the home-team Dallas Mavericks against the Los Angeles Lakers in the Western Conference semifinals on May 6, 1984.

With 31 seconds to play, the Mavs' Pat Cummings hooked in a basket to tie the score at 108 and he drew a foul from Magic Johnson. Cummings missed the free throw, but somehow teammate Harper thought he'd made it.

With 12 seconds remaining, Kareem Abdul-Jabbar missed a shot. Rolando Blackman rebounded for Dallas and tossed the ball upcourt to Dale Ellis, who flipped it to Harper. At that instant, Harper may have been the only one among millions watching on television, and at Reunion Arena, who didn't know the score.

The crowd kept yelling "Shoot!" Harper kept dribbling away and backing off toward midcourt. "Once I saw him backing up, I wanted to tackle him," said Dallas coach Dick Motta.

Then the clock ran out. Harper's mental lapse gave the Lakers the opportunity to win the game in overtime, 122-115.

In the lockerroom, Harper admitted, "Yes, I thought we were up by one. I thought Cummings had made the free throw."

It was one sad night for the rookie.

Sid Borgia's
Most Memorable Game

Sid Borgia, 5'8" and bald, was a distinctive figure among the giants of pro basketball. He refereed in the NBA from 1946 to 1966 and was later supervisor of NBA referees. He blew his whistle in more than 2,000 games, missing only one assignment in 18 years, and officiated in 8 of the league's first 14 All-Star Games.

In the first All-Star Game, at New York's Madison Square Garden, George Mikan's West team trailed by two points in the final seconds. Mikan turned to shoot and was fouled by the East's Ray Felix. Mikan went to the foul line for two shots.

Referee Borgia handed the ball to Mikan and said, "George, my old friend, you keep telling me how I choke up. Well, you've got two free throws and there are 18,000 people in this place who think you're the greatest player in creation. Let's see who gets the apple on this one."

Mikan made both foul shots to tie the score. But the West lost the game in overtime.

The Dream Team

They were called the "Dream Team," the first U.S. professional basketball players ever to compete in the Olympic Games. Indeed, in 1992 at Barcelona, Spain, the all-dream guys proved a nightmare to the opposition.

Representing the United States were the NBA's Michael Jordan, Magic Johnson, Patrick Ewing, Larry Bird, Charles Barkley, Clyde Drexler, Karl Malone, Chris Mullin, Scottie Pippen, David Robinson, and John Stockton. There was one collegian on the squad, Duke's Christian Laettner.

How could they lose? They didn't. The United States breezed to the winners' circle after having to settle for bronze as the third-place team (behind Yugoslavia and the Soviet Union) in the 1988 Olympics at Seoul, Korea. That was the year that the United States, with collegians David Robinson, Mitch Richmond, Dan Majerle, Willie Anderson, and Danny Manning heading its lineup, suffered a heartbreaking loss to the Soviets.

In all of Olympic basketball history, starting in 1936, the United States has compiled an unbelievable 90-2 record. Uncle Sam's only other setback came in 1972 at Munich, Germany, when the Soviets won after being given an extra three seconds in a controversial game.

Dream Team II

It was another first in basketball. NBA players competed as members of the United States team in the 1994 World Championships in Toronto, Canada.

Labeled as "Dream Team II," following the "Dream Team" theme of the 1992 Olympic Games, the United States lined up with Shaq O'Neal, Reggie Miller, Dominique Wilkins, Joe Dumars, Alonzo Mourning, Mark Price, Shawn Kemp, Dan Majerle, Derrick Coleman, Larry Johnson, Kevin Johnson, and Steve Smith.

It was a runaway, the United States capturing the World Championship with an 8-0 record, capped by the 137-91 gold-medal triumph over Russia.

O'Neal, the Orlando Magic superman, displayed his swooping dunks before record crowds at the SkyDome and was praised for his all-around contributions. He, Reggie Miller, and Shawn Kemp were honored by being named to the All-Tournament Team.

Basketball:
The International Pastime

Let's not hear it for soccer. In 1994 a total of 117 countries in 25 languages—from China to Guadeloupe—enjoyed television coverage of the NBA Finals.

Taking it a step further, the Portland Trail Blazers and Los Angeles Clippers launched the 1994-95 season with two games in Japan, the third time in five years the NBA has opened a season in Asia.

And in 1995-96, there will be two new teams in the NBA in Canada—the Vancouver Grizzlies and the Toronto Raptors. This will mark the first time the NBA has had a team outside of the continental limits of the United States. But once—in 1946-47—there was a team called the Toronto Huskies in the BAA (Basketball Association of America), the forerunner of the NBA.

Let's Go to the Movies

You're a basketball addict. It's raining. No shooting hoops today. No NBA game on television. What to do? Well, how about a basketball movie? Here is a list of basketball movies, many of them available at your local video store:

Above the Rim (1993): Drama about a high school basketball star trying to escape life on the mean streets and deciding to pursue a career as a ballplayer.

Blue Chips (1993): Drama about a college basketball coach (Nick Nolte) who finds himself having to break the rules in his search for players. Also with Shaquille O'Neal, Larry Bird, Bob Cousy, Anfernee Hardaway, Bobby Knight, Bobby Hurley, and Rick Pitino.

Drive, He Said (1972): A gung-ho college basketball coach (Bruce Dern) tries to solve some of his players' off-the-court problems. This was Jack Nicholson's first movie as a director.

Fast Break (1979): A comedy about a basketball coach (Gabriel Kaplan) who brings his street-smart New York City players to his new team as coach of a midwestern college.

Final Shot—The Hank Gathers Story (1993): The true story of a young basketball player (played by

Victor Love) who escaped the ghetto to become a star at Loyola Marymount College. He was destined for a big career in the NBA, but then tragedy struck.

Go, Man, Go (1954): How the Harlem Globetrotters were formed and became basketball's most magical team.

Hoop Dreams (1994): A documentary that follows the ups and downs of two young basketball players from urban Chicago. The film, shot over a seven-year period, begins with the boys at age 14 and deals with dreams of hoop gold, pressure to succeed, and how their education is neglected in the process.

Hoosiers (1986): Down on his luck, a coach (Gene Hackman) gets a last-chance job with a small-town Indiana high school team. He faces the dual challenge of winning the state championship and redeeming himself.

Maurie (1973): The touching story of how NBA star Maurice Stokes (Bernie Casey) suffers a paralyzing illness and receives care and devotion from his teammate Jack Twyman (Bo Svenson).

One on One (1977): An innocent basketball player (Robby Benson) rebels against the evils of big-time college basketball and a sadistic coach.

That Championship Season (1982): A fatherly high school coach (Robert Mitchum) has a 24th reunion with his championship team and they discover all was not as it seemed.

The Air Up There (1994): A comedy about a struggling American basketball coach (Kevin Bacon) who wants to recruit a talented young African.

The Fish That Saved Pittsburgh (1979): A comedy about a losing basketball team that tries to use astrology to get into the winner's circle. With Julius Erving, Jonathan Winters, Meadowlark Lemon, Flip Wilson, Kareem Abdul-Jabbar, and Marv Albert.

All-Star Weekend

It all started simply as an All-Star Game in 1951, pitting the best players of the East against the best of the West. But in 1984 it became more than a game. They called it All-Star Weekend, adding a Slam-Dunk Championship for the NBA's super-dunkers. In 1986, a long-distance shootout for the deadliest 3-point players was a new attraction, along with an old-timers game, which in 1994 was replaced by a game for rookies only.

Bob Pettit holds the record for most MVP awards (4) in an All-Star Game.

All-Star Game Results

Year	Result	Location	Most Valuable Player
1951	East 111, West 94	Boston	Ed Macauley, Boston
1952	East 108, West 91	Boston	Paul Arizin, Philadelphia
1953	West 79, East 75	Fort Wayne	George Mikan, Minneapolis
1954	East 98, West 93 (OT)	New York	Bob Cousy, Boston
1995	East 100, West 91	New York	Bill Sharman, Boston
1956	West 108, East 94	Rochester	Bob Pettit, St. Louis
1957	East 109, West 97	Boston	Bob Cousy, Boston
1958	East 130, West 118	St. Louis	Bob Pettit, St. Louis
1959	West 124, East 108	Detroit	Elgin Baylor, Minneapolis Bob Pettit, St. Louis
1960	East 125, West 115	Philadelphia	Wilt Chamberlain, Philadelphia

Year	Result	Host	MVP
1961	West 153, East 131	Syracuse	Oscar Robertson, Cincinnati
1962	West 150, East 130	St. Louis	Bob Pettit, St. Louis
1963	East 115, West 108	Los Angeles	Bill Russell, Boston
1964	East 111, West 107	Boston	Oscar Robertson, Cincinnati
1965	East 124, West 123	St. Louis	Jerry Lucas, Cincinnati
1966	East 127, West 94	Cincinnati	Adrian Smith, Cincinnati
1967	West 135, East 120	San Francisco	Rick Barry, San Francisco
1968	East 144, West 124	New York	Hal Greer, Philadelphia
1969	East 123, West 112	Baltimore	Oscar Robertson, Cincinnati
1970	East 142, West 135	Philadelphia	Willis Reed, New York
1971	West 108, East 107	San Diego	Lenny Wilkens, Seattle
1972	West 112, East 110	Los Angeles	Jerry West, Los Angeles
1973	East 104, West 84	Chicago	Dave Cowens, Boston
1974	West 134, East 123	Seattle	Bob Lanier, Detroit
1975	East 108, West 102	Phoenix	Walt Frazier, New York
1976	East 123, West 109	Philadelphia	Dave Bing, Washington
1977	West 125, East 124	Milwaukee	Julius Erving, Philadelphia
1978	East 133, West 125	Atlanta	Randy Smith, Buffalo
1979	West 134, East 129	Detroit	David Thompson, Denver
1980	East 144, West 135 (OT)	Washington	George Gervin, San Antonio
1981	East 123, West 120	Cleveland	Nate Archibald, Boston
1982	East 120, West 118	New Jersey	Larry Bird, Boston
1983	East 132, West 123	Los Angeles	Julius Erving, Philadelphia
1984	East 154, West 145 (OT)	Denver	Isiah Thomas, Detroit
1985	West 140, East 129	Indianapolis	Ralph Sampson, Houston
1986	East 139, West 132	Dallas	Isiah Thomas, Detroit

1987	West 154, East 149 (OT)		
		Seattle	Tom Chambers, Seattle
1988	East 138, West 133	Chicago	Michael Jordan, Chicago
1989	West 143, East 134	Houston	Karl Malone, Utah
1990	East 130, West 113	Miami	Magic Johnson, L.A. Lakers
1991	East 116, West 114	Charlotte	Charles Barkley, Philadelphia
1992	West 153, East 113	Orlando	Magic Johnson, L.A. Lakers
1993	West 135, East 132 (OT)		
		Utah	Karl Malone, Utah John Stockton, Utah
1994	East 127, West 118	Minneapolis	Scottie Pippen, Chicago

AT&T Long Distance Shootout

Year	Winner
1986	Larry Bird
1987	Larry Bird
1988	Larry Bird
1989	Dale Ellis
1990	Craig Hodges
1991	Craig Hodges
1992	Craig Hodges
1993	Mark Price
1994	Mark Price

Gatorade Slam-Dunk Championship

Year	Winner
1984	Larry Nance
1985	Dominique Wilkins
1986	Spud Webb
1987	Michael Jordan
1988	Michael Jordan
1989	Kenny Walker
1990	Dominique Wilkins
1991	Dee Brown
1992	Cedric Ceballos
1993	Harold Miner
1994	Isaiah Rider

The Draft

The best college players are chosen by the NBA teams through an annual draft. It provides a chance for the weaker teams to improve themselves. For many years, the team with the worst record in the league would draft first. Then came a change in which the teams with the two worst records would flip a coin to determine who would pick first.

In 1985 the NBA altered the method by having the teams that did not make the playoffs entered in a luck-of-the-draw lottery. That was the year the New York Knicks won the rights to the No. 1 pick, which they used to select Georgetown's Patrick Ewing.

The 1994 lottery was won by the Milwaukee Bucks, who chose Purdue's Glenn Robinson.

Though the draft started in 1947, records are incomplete until 1957. A listing of the No. 1 players taken in the draft follows:

Year	Player, College	Taken By
1957	Rod Hundley, West Virginia	Cincinnati
1958	Elgin Baylor, Seattle	Minneapolis
1959	Bob Boozer, Kansas State	Cincinnati
1960	Oscar Robertson, Cincinnati	Cincinnati
1961	Walt Bellamy, Indiana	Chicago
1962	Bill McGill, Utah	Chicago
1963	Art Heyman, Duke	New York

1964	Jim Barnes, Texas Western	New York
1965	Fred Hetzel, Davidson	San Francisco
1966	Cazzie Russell, Michigan	New York
1967	Jimmy Walker, Providence	Detroit
1968	Elvin Hayes, Houston	San Diego
1969	Kareem Abdul-Jabbar, UCLA	Milwaukee
1970	Bob Lanier, St. Bonaventure	Detroit
1971	Austin Carr, Notre Dame	Cleveland
1972	LaRue Martin, Loyola (Illinois)	Portland
1973	Doug Collins, Illinois State	Philadelphia
1974	Bill Walton, UCLA	Portland
1975	David Thompson, N. C. State	Atlanta
1976	John Lucas, Maryland	Houston
1977	Kent Benson, Indiana	Milwaukee
1978	Mychal Thompson, Minnesota	Portland
1979	Earvin Johnson, Michigan State	L.A. Lakers
1980	Joe Barry Carroll, Purdue	Golden State
1981	Mark Aguirre, DePaul	Dallas
1982	James Worthy, North Carolina	L.A. Lakers
1983	Ralph Sampson, Virginia	Houston
1984	Hakeem Olajuwon, Houston	Houston
1985	Patrick Ewing, Georgetown	New York
1986	Brad Daugherty, North Carolina	Cleveland
1987	David Robinson, Navy	San Antonio
1988	Danny Manning, Kansas	L.A. Clippers
1989	Pervis Ellison, Louisville	Sacramento
1990	Derrick Coleman, Syracuse	New Jersey
1991	Larry Johnson, Nevada-Las Vegas	Charlotte
1992	Shaquille O'Neal, Louisiana State	Orlando
1993	Chris Webber, Michigan	Orlando
1994	Glenn Robinson, Purdue	Milwaukee

Your Favorite Team

━━ ━━ ━━

You live in Boston, but you root for the San Antonio Spurs. You were born in Waukegan, Illinois, and the family moved to Miami, but you'll always be a fan of the Chicago Bulls. Whatever your team, there's one for everyone—well, 29 NBA teams—and you can look 'em up in the mini-histories that follow.

Atlanta Hawks

The Atlanta Hawks have come a long way in their illustrious history in the NBA. The team entered the league in 1949-50, when it was called the Tri-Cities Blackhawks and played its games in Iowa and Illinois. After two seasons there, the club moved to Milwaukee and shortened its nickname to Hawks. The team found its greatest success after moving to St. Louis in 1955.

For the next few seasons the Hawks were the Boston Celtics' main challengers for the NBA championship. Starting in 1957, St. Louis won five straight Western Conference titles. The Hawks advanced to the NBA Finals four times, and in 1958 won the only championship in club history by defeating the Celtics in six games in the Finals. The stars of the team were Bob Pettit, who scored 50 points in the clinching game, Cliff Hagan, Clyde Lovellette, and Slater Martin.

The Hawks enjoyed some degree of success through the early 1960s, reaching the Finals in 1960 and 1961, only to lose to the Celtics each time. The prospect of a new building in Atlanta prompted the team to move there in 1968, and the Hawks gave their new fans plenty to cheer about with stars like Lou Hudson and Pete Maravich providing thrills night after night.

Though they did not win a championship, the 1986-87 Hawks were perhaps the best team in club history. Led by dynamic Dominique Wilkins and 7-footer Kevin Willis, the Hawks finished with a record of 57-25 for first place in the Central Division. Wilkins averaged 29.0 points, second in the league behind Michael Jordan.

But the Hawks, even with homecourt advantage, could not bring a title to Atlanta. They lost to the Detroit Pistons, 4-1, in the Eastern Conference semifinals.

Over the next few seasons the scoring of Wilkins and the leadership of Glenn "Doc" Rivers kept the Hawks close to the top of the Central Division, but it wasn't until 1993-94, when former Hawk star Lenny Wilkens took over as coach, that the club showed signs of becoming a championship contender. Dominique Wilkins was traded to the Los Angeles Clippers for Danny Manning, who combined with Willis (now with Miami), Stacey Augmon, and Mookie Blaylock to help the Hawks win the Central Division with a 57-25 record. (Willis was traded to Miami in 1994 in a deal that brought Steve Smith to the Hawks.)

The Hawks lost to the Pacers in the second round of the playoffs but showed signs that their future was bright.

Bob Cousy. Bill Russell. John Havlicek. Dave Cowens. Larry Bird. With players like these, it's easy to see why the Boston Celtics are by far the most successful club in the history of professional basketball.

As a charter member of the Basketball Association of America in 1946, the Celtics struggled through some lean times in their early years. They had losing records in each of their first four seasons and failed to make the playoffs in three of those years.

Then Arnold "Red" Auerbach took over as coach, and things turned around immediately. Auerbach guided the Celtics to a 16 $1/2$-game improvement (22-46 to 39-30). The arrival of rookie guard Bob Cousy in 1951 made the Celtics contenders and the acquisition of shot-blocking wizard Bill Russell in 1956 made them champions.

Russell's arrival changed the NBA game as defense and shot-blocking became keys to winning. The Celtics won the NBA title in 1956-57, Russell's rookie year, by outlasting the St. Louis Hawks, 125-123, in double overtime of Game 7 at Boston Garden. They lost the title to the Hawks the following year when Russell hurt his ankle in the Finals, but then won again in 1958, starting an incredible run of eight consecutive championships.

The Celtics of Russell, Cousy, Tommy Heinsohn, Satch Sanders, and Sam and K.C. Jones dominated the league through the first half of the 1960s. And when they needed help, Auerbach traded well (picking up Don Nelson) and drafted Havlicek.

Auerbach handed over the coaching reins to Russell in 1966 and the Celtics' streak of titles was ended by the Philadelphia 76ers. But Boston regrouped and won two more titles (1968, 1969). Heinsohn took over for Russell after the second title and, with Dave Cowens in the middle, led the team to championships in 1974 and 1976.

The Celtics, with a corps of All-Stars in Bird, Kevin McHale, Robert Parish, and Dennis Johnson, went on to win three more championships in the 1980s. That gave them 16 titles, five more than their closest franchise competitor, the Lakers (Minneapolis, Los Angeles).

Bzzzz. That's the sound that blares over the public-address system at the Charlotte Coliseum when opponents have the ball. Not that the Coliseum needs any more sound; the hometown Charlotte Hornets have given the fans much to yell about in a very short time.

The Hornets entered the league in 1988-89, joining the Miami Heat as expansion teams. The fans in Charlotte, who follow college basketball with a passion, fell in love with their new team immediately, but that enthusiasm did not translate into many wins on the court at first.

Led by Kelly Tripucka, mighty mite Muggsy Bogues, Dell Curry, and Rex Chapman, the Hornets entertained their fans with fast-paced basketball. Their enthusiasm under coach Dick Harter and the support they received from their home fans paid off in 20 victories, five games better than the Heat.

But Charlotte fans had to learn to be patient, and that patience was tested in 1989-90 when the club started with five straight losses and finished with a 19-63 mark. Still, sellout crowds of 23,900 continued to pack Charlotte Coliseum night after night.

The real excitement in Charlotte started in 1991-92 when rookie Larry Johnson of Nevada-Las Vegas came aboard. Johnson, an accurate shooter and powerful rebounder, stepped into the starting lineup immediately, averaging 19 points and 11 rebounds, and provided the inside game the Hornets needed. They stayed in playoff contention until March, but 11 losses in their last 14 games kept them out of postseason play.

But by not making the playoffs the Hornets wound up with a lottery pick, which they used on Georgetown center Alonzo Mourning. The 6'10" rookie averaged 21 points, 10.3 rebounds and 3.5 blocks as he helped the Hornets improve to a 44-38 record and claim their first-ever playoff berth in 1992-93. They stung the Boston Celtics in the first round before losing to the Knicks in the Eastern Conference semifinals.

Injuries to Johnson and Mourning hurt Charlotte in 1993-94, when the Hornets failed to make the playoffs, but the young team has a bright future.

CHICAGO

CHICAGO BULLS

Three-peat. That was the Chicago Bulls' motto in 1992-93 as they tried to become only the third team in NBA history to win three straight championships. But standing in their way on the night of June 20, 1993, were the Phoenix Suns, who had stunned the basketball world by winning Game 5 in Chicago two nights before, cutting the Bulls' lead in the series to three games to two. Now, back in Phoenix for Game 6, the Suns had a 98-94 lead with just over a minute left.

Michael Jordan gave the Bulls hope when he scored on a driving layup, and then Chicago's tough defense forced a 24-second violation, giving the Bulls one last chance. Who would take the shot? Would it be Jordan, the game's greatest player? Or would it be Scottie Pippen, who already had 23 points and 12 rebounds?

Instead, with the clock running down, the Bulls got the ball to Horace Grant near the basket. But Grant, who had scored only one point in the game, immediately fired it back to John Paxson, who was standing just outside the 3-point line on the left side. Paxson never hesitated, firing up a shot that swished through the basket with 3.9 seconds left. The Bulls had their three-peat.

Chicago joined the league in 1966 and surprisingly made the playoffs that season, winning 33 games under coach Johnny "Red" Kerr.

The appointment of Dick Motta as coach in 1968 brought a change in styles for the Bulls. Motta stressed tough team defense and soon they were among the league's best at holding teams under 100 points. That strategy worked as the Bulls, with Bob Love and Chet Walker, won 50 games or more four seasons in a row from 1971 through 1974. Included in that stretch was the Bulls' first-ever playoff series victory, a 7-game elimination of Detroit in 1974.

The Bulls did not win another playoff series until 1981 and did not advance to the conference finals until 1989. By that time, they had made the most important move in team history—the selection of Jordan with the third pick in the 1984 Draft. The former North Carolina star took the league by storm, averaging 28.2 points in his rookie season and thrilling fans all over the league with his incredible moves and dunks.

Jordan went on to lead the league in scoring seven straight times and, of course, take the team to those three consecutive championships under coach Phil Jackson.

CAVS™

Unfortunately for the Cavaliers, what could have been the greatest moment in their history turned into the most disappointing.

It was May 7, 1989, and the Cavaliers were playing the Chicago Bulls in the final game of an Eastern Conference playoff series. The Cavaliers, led by Brad Daugherty and Mark Price, had kept their season alive with a 108-105 overtime win at Chicago Stadium two days earlier. Now they were playing for the right to advance in the playoffs.

As the seconds wound down, the Cavaliers held a 100-99 lead, but the Bulls had the ball. They set up a play for Michael Jordan, who was covered closely by Craig Ehlo. With the buzzer about to sound, Jordan cut toward the foul line and went up for a shot. Ehlo followed with him, but Jordan stayed up a split-second longer and arched the ball just over Ehlo's reach. The ball swished through the basket, giving the Bulls the triumph that ended the Cavaliers' season.

Cleveland entered the NBA in 1970-71 and struggled to a 15-67 record, the worst in the league. Under coach Bill Fitch, the team had 23 wins the next season, 32 the year after that.

The move to a new arena in Richfield, Ohio, and the additions of center Jim Chones and forward Campy Russell helped the Cavaliers in 1975-76. They played stifling defense, limiting opponents to an average of under 100 points per game, and crowds poured into the Coliseum to watch a team that finished with a 49-33 record. In their first playoff series in club history, Cleveland eliminated the Washington Bullets in seven games. Then they took the eventual champion Boston Celtics to six games before losing.

The Cavaliers would not win another playoff series until 1991-92, when after a 57-25 regular season, they defeated the New Jersey Nets and Boston Celtics in back-to-back series before Jordan and his Bulls eliminated them again in the Eastern Conference Finals.

In 1992-93, the Cavaliers reached the Eastern Conference semifinals, only to be ousted once more by the Bulls. They didn't make the playoffs in 1993-94, but they had a change of address in 1994-95—the new Gund Arena in Cleveland.

**DALLAS
MAVERICKS**

™

Dallas may be in the Lone Star State, but the Dallas Mavericks certainly have had more than one star during their existence in the NBA. The Mavericks entered the league as an expansion franchise in 1980-81 and came in with a bang, winning their first game, 103-92, over the eventual Midwest Division champion San Antonio Spurs.

But they won only 14 more games the rest of the season. One of them, a 105-95 come-from-behind victory over Utah, prompted coach Dick Motta to say, "This is the best group of pros I ever worked with. I don't think in 20 years I'll be able to say I've ever had a better bunch."

That bunch got better the following season. The Mavericks used their first two picks in the draft to take DePaul's Mark Aguirre and Kansas State's Rolando Blackman, two players who would make their marks. Though Aguirre missed two months of the season with an injury, the Mavericks finished with a 28-54 record, a 13-game improvement over their first year.

The 1982-83 season was a downer, but with the presence of rookies Dale Ellis and Derek Harper, the

Mavericks took second in the Midwest Division in 1983-84.

Rookies Sam Perkins came aboard in 1984 and Roy Tarpley in 1986, and it was in 1986-87 that Dallas won the Midwest Division with its best record ever, 55-27. But the Mavericks were ousted in the first round of the playoffs by Seattle.

Under new coach John MacLeod in 1987-88, Dallas was 53-29 and on a roll with a team led by Blackman and Aguirre. The Mavericks eliminated Houston and Denver in the playoffs, but fell to the Los Angeles Lakers in a 7-game Western Conference Finals.

It has been downhill since then, with the exception of 1989-90, when Dallas won 47 games and made the first round of the playoffs. The Mavericks won only 11 games in 1992-93 and 13 in 1993-94. But the arrival of Jim Jackson in 1992, Jamal Mashburn in 1993, and Jason Kidd in 1994, along with the return of coach Motta, have given the Mavs new hope.

From red, white, and blue to young, brash, and exciting, the Nuggets' history goes back to the tri-colored ball of the American Basketball Association and follows through to the 1993-94 team that became the talk of the NBA with its playoff success.

Those Nuggets, under coach and former NBA player Dan Issel, were a tough, fearless team that very nearly made it to the Western Conference Finals. Issel toned down the fast-breaking style the club was known for in the late 1980s and, instead, put in an offense that made the most of the abilities of 7-foot Dikembe Mutombo and Mahmoud Abdul-Rauf.

Mutombo averaged only 12 points a game, but finished second in the league in field-goal percentage, was sixth in rebounds, and led the NBA in blocks. He was also the key man in a defense that allowed only 98.8 points per game.

Issel's 1993-94 Nuggets qualified for the playoffs with a 42-40 record but no one gave them much of a chance against Seattle, seeded No. 1 in the conference after posting a 63-19 mark. After losing the first two games in Seattle, Mutombo, Abdul-Rauf, LaPhonso

Ellis and Co. came back to win the series in Game 5.

The Western Conference semifinals against Utah looked like a mismatch as the Nuggets dropped the first three games. But they rallied for three straight victories before yielding to the Jazz.

Based on its youth and talent—and the addition of rookie Jalen Rose of Michigan—Denver entered the 1994-95 season on a note of optimism.

The team's history began in the ABA in 1967-68, when they were nicknamed the Rockets. The early days were highlighted by such stars as Ralph Simpson, Mack Calvin, and Larry Jones. Larry Brown became coach in 1974-75, when the Rockets became Nuggets, and he led them to a 65-19 mark and the Western Conference Finals. The addition of David Thompson and Issel in 1975-76 enabled Denver to reach the ABA Finals, where they lost to Julius Erving and his New York Nets.

That was the last season of the ABA, with Denver, the Nets, Indiana, and San Antonio joining the NBA the following year. From then until 1993-94, Denver evolved into a team known for its run-and-gun style that produced not only record numbers of points but also record numbers of points allowed.

Did you ever wonder how a team could be nicknamed the Pistons? Well, when your name is Fred Zollner, president of the Zollner Piston Company, and you own the club, you can call it anything you want. So when Zollner founded the franchise in Fort Wayne, Indiana, in 1948, he named the team the Fort Wayne Zollner Pistons.

Little did he know that his team would be greatly responsible for the way the game is played in the 1990s. Before the Detroit Pistons of the late 1980s started winning consistently, most NBA teams stressed offense, averaging between 105 and 110 points per game. Coach Chuck Daly knew his Pistons did not have the firepower to keep up with the NBA's better teams, so he had his teams play a tough, swarming defense that many teams copied in later years.

The Pistons were known as the "Bad Boys" because of their aggressiveness on defense and their physical play at both ends of the court. Daly rotated three guards—Isiah Thomas, Joe Dumars, and Vinnie Johnson—with a strong frontcourt that featured center Bill Laimbeer and forwards Rick Mahorn, Dennis Rodman, and John Salley.

Were they successful? You bet. The 1987-88 Pistons came within a whisker of winning the championship. They held a 3-game-to-2 lead on the Los Angeles Lakers in the Finals, but lost Games 6 and 7 in Los Angeles by a combined four points.

The Pistons came into the 1988-89 season determined not to let it happen again. The result was one of the greatest seasons any NBA team ever enjoyed. The Pistons coasted to a 63-19 regular-season record and then rolled through the playoffs.

They swept Boston in three games and Milwaukee in four before running into a challenge from Chicago. They lost two of the first three games to the Michael Jordan-led Bulls before winning three straight. The Lakers again waited for them in the Finals, but this time it was no contest. The Pistons won four straight games to nail down their first championship. They didn't have to wait long for their second, as Daly again led them to the 1990 title with a 5-game triumph over Portland in the Finals.

The success erased the stigma of mediocrity that had followed the club from Fort Wayne through its days at Cobo Hall in downtown Detroit. Though there were some great individual talents (George Yardley, Dave Bing, Bob Lanier) the Pistons never enjoyed much success until Daly took over in 1983-84.

Detroit, which faded back to the pack after winning two titles, was hoping No. 3 draft pick Grant Hill would herald another period of success.

From their start in Philadelphia as an original Basketball Association of America franchise in 1946-47, the Warriors have been a team with a rich tradition. That tradition started when their first team, the Philadelphia Warriors, led by league scoring champion Joe Fulks, won the BAA championship by defeating the Chicago Stags. They won another championship in 1956, then made the move that made the team a contender for years: the signing of center Wilt Chamberlain in 1959.

Chamberlain became the sport's biggest star in his first year with the Warriors. That season he shattered all scoring records by averaging 37.6 points and helping the Warriors improve from 32 to 49 wins. Two years later, Chamberlain averaged a staggering 50.4 points.

Unfortunately for the Warriors, Chamberlain's individual brilliance did not lead to championships because Bill Russell and the Boston Celtics stood in the way. The Celtics ended the Warriors' season three times in a 5-year span, and not even a move to San Francisco could change the Warriors' luck.

The Warriors traded Chamberlain to the Philadelphia 76ers in the middle of the 1964-65 season in a shocking deal. The move backfired two years later when Chamberlain led the 76ers to the championship in six games over the Warriors, whose star player was a young forward named Rick Barry.

There were bright moments coming, though. Former Warrior star Al Attles took over as coach late in 1969-70. Barry, who had left the Warriors to join the ABA in 1967, rejoined the team in 1972 and his scoring, playmaking, and defense helped them achieve their greatest triumph in 1975. Barry averaged 30.6 points and 6.2 assists as the Warriors posted a 48-34 record and then defeated Seattle and Chicago to advance to the Finals against the Washington Bullets.

Most experts figured the Bullets would handle the young Warriors, but it didn't happen. With Barry scoring almost at will and feeding Keith Wilkes and Butch Beard, the Warriors stunned the Bullets in four straight games for their only championship since leaving for the West Coast.

The Warriors had a long drought thereafter. Out of the playoffs for a decade, they made it to the second round in 1987 with Eric Floyd, Joe Barry Carroll, and Chris Mullin, who has been the team's mainstay since then. The arrival of Tim Hardaway in 1989 and Latrell Sprewell, Chris Webber, and Billy Owens more recently have kept them competitive and exciting. Webber, the 1994 NBA Rookie of the Year, became an ex-Warrior early in the 1994-95 season when he was traded to the Washington Bullets for Tom Gugliotta and first-round draft picks in 1996, 1998, and 2000. Billy Owens was also traded in 1994, to Miami for Rony Seikaly, the center the Warriors had hoped for for years.

Hakeem Olajuwon's nickname is "The Dream," and his dream in 1993-94 was to bring the city of Houston its first NBA championship.

Olajuwon had come out of the University of Houston in 1984 and his agility, quickness, and shot-blocking immediately made him one of the league's best centers. In only his second season, he averaged 23.5 points, 11.5 rebounds, and 3.4 blocks and led the Rockets into the 1986 Finals, where they were defeated by the Boston Celtics in six games.

It took eight years for Olajuwon and the Rockets to get back to the Finals. Olajuwon averaged 27.3 points, 11.9 rebounds, and 3.71 blocks as he led the Rockets to a league-best 58-24 record. In the playoffs, Houston easily disposed of Portland in the first round, but in the next round lost the first two games at home to the Phoenix Suns.

With their own hometown papers calling them "chokers," the Rockets responded. They battled back to defeat the Suns in seven games, then eliminated the Utah Jazz to reach the Finals against the New York Knicks. The Finals were billed as the battle of the big men, Hakeem vs. Patrick Ewing, and it was Olajuwon who won the battle and the championship. His two free throws and block in the final seconds of Game 6 enabled the Rockets to force a seventh game, and then he had 25 points, 10 rebounds, and 7 assists in the Rockets' 90-84 victory in Game 7.

The Rockets' long journey to the top of the NBA began in San Diego in 1967. The expansion Rockets won only 15 of 82 games their first season, but that earned them the right to choose first in the 1968 Draft. They used that pick to take Elvin Hayes, a 6'9" sharpshooter who had starred at the University of Houston. All Hayes did was average 28.4 points and 17.1 rebounds, helping the Rockets improve by 22 games. But the Rockets never really caught on in San Diego and the team moved to Houston in 1971.

Center Moses Malone took the Rockets to the Finals in 1981 and Olajuwon did the same five years later, but both times Houston was beaten by the Larry Bird-led Celtics in six games. In 1994, no one could stop them.

INDIANA

Pacers®

The three biggest things in the state of Indiana every winter are high school basketball, Indiana University basketball, and the Indiana Pacers. In that order. But the 1993-94 edition of the Pacers indicated that the order may be changing. After years of either not making the playoffs or making them but then going out quietly, those Pacers finally took the step to becoming contenders for the championship.

Coach Larry Brown assembled a young, aggressive group that became the hottest team in the NBA down the stretch as they rolled to a 47-35 regular-season record. Reggie Miller, one of the league's most dangerous 3-point shooters, and center Rik Smits gave the Pacers a strong 1-2 scoring punch, and Dale Davis and Derrick McKey provided rebounding strength few teams could match.

The first round of the playoffs brought the challenge of Shaquille O'Neal and the Orlando Magic, but the Pacers won in three straight games. Next came the Atlanta Hawks, who had earned the Eastern Conference's top seed with a 57-25 record. Again, it was no contest as the Pacers came through in six games.

Waiting for the Pacers in the Eastern Conference Finals were the New York Knicks, who had eliminated the Pacers from the playoffs in 1993. The Pacers immediately dropped the first two games in New York but bounced back to win two in Indiana and tie the series. Game 5 was to be Reggie Miller's night. The flamboyant guard took over a close game in the fourth quarter, pouring in 25 points as the Pacers stunned the Knicks and moved within a game of advancing to the Finals for the first time.

But it wasn't to be. The Knicks won Games 6 and 7 and went on to the Finals.

Still, the Pacers' effort won them the kind of support they used to have in the old American Basketball Association days. Those teams—led by Roger Brown, Mel Daniels, and Freddie Lewis—dominated the ABA, winning three championships in a span of four years.

The transition to the NBA in 1976 was a rough one as the Pacers did not win a playoff series until the memorable run of 1994.

LOS ANGELES CLIPPERS ®

Move over, Lakers. You'll have to share Los Angeles. That seemed to be the message the Los Angeles Clippers were sending in the early 1990s.

After years of playing second fiddle while the Lakers were becoming the NBA's dominant team of the 1980s, the Clippers made the rest of the league notice them in 1991-92. With Ron Harper and Mark Jackson forming an explosive backcourt, and Danny Manning and Ken Norman providing the in-close points and rebounds, the Clippers became a legitimate playoff contender. A midseason coaching switch to Larry Brown helped, too, as the Clippers finished at 45-37, ahead of their arch-rival Lakers for the first time. This gave the Clippers their first playoff berth since 1975-76, when the team was based in Buffalo.

In 1992-93, Manning became one of the league's brightest stars, averaging 22.8 points, and Harper chipped in with 18.0 points and 4.5 assists as the Clippers finished 41-41. In the playoffs they gave No. 2 seed Houston all it could handle before dropping an 84-80 decision in the fifth game at the Summit.

The 1993-94 season was one of change for the

Clippers. Manning, who would have been a free agent at the end of the season, was traded to Atlanta for Dominique Wilkins. Wilkins averaged 29.1 points in his 25 games with the Clippers but was unable to salvage what would wind up as a 27-55 season.

Some of the Clippers' brightest days came in the very beginning, when they were based in Buffalo and were known as the Braves. They entered the league in 1970 and, within five years, became a contender. The turning point came in the 1972 Draft when the Braves added Bob McAdoo, a 6'9" jump-shooting machine who quickly became a fixture among the league leaders in scoring.

With McAdoo averaging 30.6 points per game, the 1973-74 Braves finished 42-40, then took the powerful Boston Celtics to six games before losing in the playoffs. The next season the Braves won a club-record 49 games, and in the playoffs took the Washington Bullets to seven games before falling.

The 1975-76 Braves hold the honor as the only team in franchise history to win a playoff series. McAdoo averaged 31.1 points as the team finished 46-36, then ousted the 76ers in the first round. But a loss to the Celtics followed, and three years later the Braves were on their way to San Diego.

Los Angeles is not known for its lakes, but the state of Minnesota is, and that's how a team based in L.A. ended up with a nickname borrowed from another state at another time. The original Lakers played in Minneapolis and entered the NBA in 1949. It didn't take long for the club to build a tradition of excellence as George Mikan, the first of the NBA's great big men, led the team to the league championship in its first season. Mikan's dominance made the Lakers the league's first dynasty, with five championships in a 6-year stretch.

The Lakers gave the NBA its first presence on the West Coast when they moved to Los Angeles for the 1960-61 season. If not for the Boston Celtics, the Lakers of the 1960s might have duplicated the success of the early Minneapolis teams. But the Celtics defeated the Lakers in the Finals six times in an 8-year span. Those Laker teams, which featured Elgin Baylor and Jerry West, became known as some of the greatest never to win a title. Not even a trade for Wilt Chamberlain in 1968 could change the Lakers' fortune in the Finals.

The first West Coast title finally came in 1972. Chamberlain combined with West, Gail Goodrich, Jim McMillian, and Happy Hairston on a team that set an NBA record with 33 straight wins in the regular season and then coasted through the playoffs, winning 12 of 15 games.

The retirement of West, Baylor, and Chamberlain led to some down years but the Lakers recovered by trading with Milwaukee for Kareem Abdul-Jabbar in 1975. The 7'2" center, who would become the game's all-time leading scorer, kept the Lakers respectable until the drafting of Earvin "Magic" Johnson in 1979. The 6'9" Johnson immediately became the league's tallest and most dangerous point guard. He even filled in at center for Game 6 of the 1980 Finals against the 76ers, and his 42 points led the Lakers to their first championship in eight years.

The Lakers' fast-breaking style became known as Showtime, and Los Angeles became known as the Titletown of the NBA. With Abdul-Jabbar and Johnson joined by James Worthy and Byron Scott, the Lakers went on to win four more championships in the 1980s. They even ended the hex of the arch-rival Celtics when they defeated them in a 6-game Finals in 1985. The duels between Johnson and Larry Bird, the Celtics' star who also joined the NBA in 1979, became some of the most exciting in history.

Johnson retired in 1991, leaving the Lakers with a large hole in their lineup. But the play of Vlade Divac and youngsters Nick Van Exel, Anthony Peeler, and Cedric Ceballos, and rookie Eddie Jones provided hope in 1994-95.

The story of the Miami Heat can be summed up in one word: patience. As the team prepared to start its first season in 1988, management decided to go with the youngest club possible and build through the draft rather than add veterans who might help immediately but who wouldn't be around for the long run.

The Heat's strategy paid off, but not in the first season. The 1988-89 Heat lost their first 17 games while rookies Rony Seikaly and Kevin Edwards gained valuable experience. Though the team finished with only 15 wins, Seikaly and Edwards provided a foundation to build on.

Glen Rice and Sherman Douglas were added in the 1989 Draft, and each was given plenty of playing time in an 18-64 season that was ruined by a 13-game losing streak in December and January. But still the Heat remained patient, knowing that their top four scorers were either first-or second-year players. The fans at Miami Arena continued to support the club, which sold out each of its 41 home games.

Willie Burton (1990) and Steve Smith (1991) joined the Heat in the next two Drafts, and now all the pieces were in place for a run at a playoff spot. With Rice's long-range shooting and Seikaly's inside game providing a 1-2 punch, the 1991-92 Heat won 28 of 41 home games to finish at 38-44 and earn the team's first playoff spot. A highlight was Rice's 46 points in a late-season win over Orlando. That the Heat lost three straight games to the eventual champion Bulls hardly mattered; what was important was that the Heat had stepped up their game and made it into post-season play.

After not making the playoffs in 1992-93, the Heat had its best season in 1993-94, finishing over .500 (42-40) for the first time. The core of the team was Rice, Smith, and Seikaly, and they weren't satisfied with simply making the playoffs this time. They threw a giant scare into the East's top seed, Atlanta, in the first round before losing in five games. But now everyone in the NBA knew the Heat was here to stay. While the departure of Steve Smith (traded to Atlanta) and Rony Seikaly (traded to the Warriors) in 1994 was a major change to the Heat lineup, the addition of Kevin Willis and Billy Owens will no doubt keep the Heat on the rise.

MILWAUKEE

No team in any professional sport made a faster impact than the Milwaukee Bucks did in the early 1970s. And they did it mostly because of a coin flip.

The team entered the NBA as an expansion franchise in 1968-69 and suffered through growing pains. A 27-55 record left them in last place in the Eastern Division but put them in position to draft Kareem Abdul-Jabbar of UCLA, the most dominant college player of his generation. To get the rights to Abdul-Jabbar, all the Bucks would have to do was win a coin flip with the Phoenix Suns, who also entered the league that season and had finished in last place in the Western Division.

The Suns called heads, the coin came up tails, and Abdul-Jabbar was on his way to Milwaukee. The 7'2" center's impact on the league was incredible. The Bucks went from 27 to 56 wins and challenged the New York Knicks for the Eastern Division title while Abdul-Jabbar finished second in the league in scoring (28.8) and third in rebounds (13.5).

As it turned out, the young Bucks didn't have enough to win a championship. They defeated the

Philadelphia 76ers in the first round of the 1970 playoffs but were beaten by the Knicks in the Eastern Conference Finals. The defeat convinced the Bucks they needed one more superstar to reach the top. During the off-season, that superstar came when the Bucks acquired Oscar Robertson from the Cincinnati Royals.

The Robertson-Abdul-Jabbar combination quickly proved to be too much for the rest of the NBA. In 1970-71, the Bucks finished with a league-best 66-16 record and won the Midwest Division by a whopping 15 games. In the playoffs, the Bucks romped past San Francisco and Los Angeles before blowing out the Baltimore Bullets in four straight in the Finals. That gave the Bucks the championship in only their third season, faster than any team in any professional sport.

The next season, the Bucks didn't get beyond the Western Conference Finals, losing to the Lakers. Two years later, in 1974, they almost won a second title, Boston taking the Bucks in Game 7.

Even after the departure of Abdul-Jabbar to Los Angeles in a 1975 trade, the Bucks went on to dominate the Central Division. With Sidney Moncrief and Terry Cummings, they won six straight division crowns from 1980-81 through 1985-86. They went to the Conference Finals three times, only to lose each time.

New coach Mike Dunleavy started rebuilding the team in the early 1990s, bringing in Todd Day, Eric Murdock, and Vin Baker. Murdock has become one of the NBA's best young guards.

The 1994 drafting of Purdue's Glenn Robinson, No. 1 overall, is expected to have a marked effect on the Bucks.

Never has an NBA team ever attracted more fan support than the Minnesota Timberwolves did in 1989-90, their first season. Playing in the spacious Metrodome while waiting for their own arena to be built, the Timberwolves attracted 1,072,572 fans to their home games, a per-game average of 26,160.

The fans showed their support of a defense-oriented club that won only 22 times, but held its opponents to an average of only 99.4 points. Offensively, the star was Tony Campbell, a veteran forward who had arrived in the expansion draft and averaged 23.2 points.

Campbell was nearly as strong the following season and his teammates were more effective. They won six of their final eight games to finish at 29-53.

But in 1991-92 the T-Wolves struggled to a 4-23 mark in the first two months of the season and then a 16-game losing streak later in the campaign ensured that they would have their worst record ever. The bright spot was that Minnesota wound up with the third pick in the lottery and they used that on Duke All-American Christian Laettner, a 6'11" forward who had been the first collegian in history to start in four

NCAA Tournament Final Fours.

The addition of Laettner, the improvement of Doug West, and a preseason trade with Indiana that brought in Chuck Person and Michael Williams made the T-Wolves much more competitive in 1992-93. Laettner was named to the All-Rookie Team after averaging 18.2 points and 8.7 assists and West, in his fourth season, averaged a career-high 19.3 points as the T-Wolves finished at 19-63. One highlight was Williams breaking Calvin Murphy's NBA record by making 84 consecutive free throws in the final month.

The 1993 Draft brought in Isaiah (J.R.) Rider from Nevada-Las Vegas and he combined with Laettner to give Minnesota one of the best young frontcourts in the league. Rider, who won the Slam-Dunk contest at the All-Star Weekend, averaged 16.6 points, second on the club behind Laettner's 16.8, and the T-Wolves improved to 20-62. Williams, meanwhile, extended his streak of consecutive free throws to 97 before missing early in the 1993-94 season.

The T-Wolves got new ownership before the 1994-95 season that avoided a shift of the franchise to New Orleans. They also got a promising rookie, Connecticut's Donyell Marshall, in the draft.

The New Jersey Nets have been a saga of triumph and tragedy since they came into the NBA as one of the four American Basketball Association franchises in 1976. Much of the triumph came in the mid-1970s, when the team was still in the ABA and based on Long Island as the New York Nets. The Nets had put together a team built around forward Julius Erving, a local product who was the most spectacular player of his generation.

Dr. J was known for his incredible leaping ability and soaring dunks. The Nets took full advantage of his ability, using a fast-break style that often ended in a windmill slam dunk by Erving. With Larry Kenon at the other forward, Billy Paultz at center, and John Williamson at guard, the Nets built a team that won two of the last three ABA championships.

But a contract dispute prompted owner Roy Boe to send Erving to the 76ers before the Nets' first NBA season started in 1976, and the team's hopes of competing in the expanded league vanished. After a 22-60 record, Boe moved the team to New Jersey, where the fans had the pleasure of seeing rookie

Bernard King average 24.2 points and 9.5 rebounds.

The early 1980s were the Nets' finest years in the NBA. With young forward Buck Williams and Albert King playing alongside dynamic center Darryl Dawkins, the Nets made the playoffs five straight times.

The 1983-84 team was the only one to win a playoff series, though, and it was memorable. The Nets won 19 of their last 25 games, then stunned the defending champion Philadelphia 76ers in the first round of the playoffs. Their season was ended by the Milwaukee Bucks in the next round.

But a series of injuries ruined the Nets in the late 1980s. Dawkins, Otis Birdsong, Keith Lee, and Joe Barry Carroll were all sidelined by major ailments and the Nets' hopes skidded.

Just when it seemed the Nets were turning things around, tragedy struck. The team had rebuilt behind forward Derrick Coleman and guard Kenny Anderson and made the playoffs in both 1992 and 1993. But after the 1992-93 season, starting guard Drazen Petrovic was killed in an automobile accident, leaving the Nets with a huge hole to fill.

Despite the tragic loss, the 1993-94 Nets managed to make the playoffs and throw a scare into the Knicks in a tough, 4-game series in the first round.

The New York Knicks, who entered the league as one of its charter members in 1946, have had many proud moments in their long tenure, but none was prouder than the night of May 7, 1970. It was on that night that Willis Reed led them to their first NBA championship.

It was Game 7 of the Finals between the Knicks and the Los Angeles Lakers, and the Knicks knew their hopes of winning the title depended on the condition of their 6'10" center and captain. Reed had injured his hip in a collision in Game 5 and no one knew if he would be ready to return for the decisive seventh game. The Knicks had battled back without Reed to win Game 5 but were routed in Game 6 in Los Angeles, tying the series.

The teams came out to warm up for Game 7, but there was no Reed. Not even the other Knicks knew if he'd be playing. Suddenly, about five minutes before tipoff, a roar went up from the crowd. They had spotted Reed coming through the tunnel onto the court. The inspired Knicks knew there was no stopping them now. Their center hit his first two shots to stake them to an early lead, and then Walt Frazier chipped in with 36 points and 19 assists to propel the Knicks to a 113-99 victory and their first NBA championship.

That title erased years of frustration for the Knicks, who had made it to the Finals three straight times in the early 1950s, only to lose each time. After winning in 1970, the Knicks challenged for another title the next three years, losing in the Finals in 1972, then winning over the Lakers in 1973.

After some down years, the Knicks started rebuilding in 1985, with a little luck. In the NBA's first lottery, they won the right to draft Georgetown center Patrick Ewing, who would go on to become one of the league's most dominant big men.

Ewing played only 50 games his rookie season due to injuries but still averaged 20 points and 9 rebounds. Ewing's presence helped the Knicks make the playoffs in his third season, and then trades for Charles Oakley and Charles Smith, and the improvement of former CBA players John Starks and Anthony Mason made the Knicks serious contenders in the 1990s.

They lost to the eventual champion Chicago Bulls in both the 1992 and 1993 playoffs and then were beaten by the Houston Rockets in a stirring 7-game Finals in 1994.

If there's one thing the Orlando Magic have proven in their short stay in the NBA, it's that they play the lottery game very well. The Magic was part of the NBA Lottery two straight years, and both times the team wound up with the No. 1 pick in the draft.

The first time, 1992, the Magic picked 7'1" center Shaquille O'Neal of Louisiana State. O'Neal, whose game was built around his brute strength, had a sensational rookie season, finishing eighth in the league in scoring (23.4), second in rebounds (13.4), and second in blocks (3.53). But not even the presence of the awesome O'Neal could get the Magic into the playoffs.

However, by not getting into postseason play, the Magic again qualified for the Lottery. And though they were the least likely of 11 teams to get the No. 1 pick, they defied the odds and won it in 1993. They used the pick on Michigan's Chris Webber, then traded him to the Golden State Warriors for the rights to guard Anfernee "Penny" Hardaway and three first-round picks. So in the space of two years the Magic had obtained a dominating center, an exciting, young point guard, and enough first-round picks to keep them competitive for years.

O'Neal was even more dominating in his second season. After taking time out from basketball in the summer to record a rap album and star in the movie *Blue Chips*, Shaq came back and averaged 29.3 points and 13.2 rebounds. He would have won the scoring title if not for a 71-point effort by the Spurs' David Robinson on the final day of the season. Hardaway, meanwhile, chipped in with 16.0 points, 6.6 assists, and 2.32 steals per game.

This time there was no doubt about making the playoffs. The Magic rolled to a 50-32 record, only seven games behind the Atlantic Division-leading Knicks, and earned a playoff spot against the Indiana Pacers.

The Pacers' experience proved to be too much for the young Magic, though. Indiana won two close games at Orlando Arena, then wrapped up the series with a win in Indiana.

The city of Philadelphia has always been known for the Liberty Bell, cheesesteaks, and pretzels with mustard. And for much of the past 30 years it's been known for good basketball, too.

The 76ers are one of the NBA's charter franchises. They started play as the Syracuse Nationals in the Basketball Association of America in 1946. Those days in Syracuse were memorable for the crowds, who used to involve themselves in the action by shaking the guidewires to the basket while a Nationals' opponent was shooting free throws.

Not that the Nationals needed that much help; the 1954-55 team, led by forward Dolph Schayes (whose son Dan would later play in the NBA), won the league championship with a 7-game triumph over the Fort Wayne Pistons. The club moved to the City of Brotherly Love in 1963, partly to fill the void left by the Philadelphia Warriors, who had moved to San Francisco.

Once in Philadelphia, the Nationals renamed themselves the 76ers and started building one of the toughest teams in the NBA. Two years after the move, the 76ers stunned the NBA by obtaining Wilt Chamberlain from the Warriors in a multi-player deal. The addition of Chamberlain to a team that already had Hal Greer, Lucius Jackson, and Chet Walker made the 76ers championship contenders.

The 1966-67 team, which is regarded as one of the great teams in NBA history, broke through the Celtics' domination and ended their streak of eight straight championships. Chamberlain averaged "only" 24 points but contributed 24 rebounds and 7.8 assists per game as the 76ers won 68 of 81 games then ousted Cincinnati, Boston, and San Francisco to bring the championship to Philadelphia.

The 76ers had to wait 16 years for another title. The 1982-83 team, led by Julius Erving and Moses Malone, had a league-best 65-17 record in the regular season. Malone said before the playoffs that the 76ers would win in "four, four, and four" and he was nearly right. The team dropped only 1 of 13 games in rolling to the title over New York, Milwaukee, and Los Angeles.

The 76ers have not come close to winning another title since then, despite the presence of Charles Barkley from 1984-85 through 1991-92. But in 1994-95, they were looking for a turnaround with a team featuring such young hopefuls as 7'6" center Shawn Bradley, Clarence Weatherspoon, and their top '94 Draft choice, Clemson's Sharone Wright.

Say one thing for the Phoenix Suns: when they make it to the NBA Finals, you know it will be a memorable series.

Take 1992-93, for example. The Suns, led by Charles Barkley and Kevin Johnson, rolled to an NBA-best 62-20 regular-season record and then disposed of the Lakers, Spurs, and SuperSonics en route to a date with the Michael Jordan-led Chicago Bulls in the Finals.

The series looked like a rout in the early stages as the Bulls, who were seeking their third straight championship, won Games 1 and 2. "We're in a big hole right now, and we're in the right state for big holes," Barkley said after Game 2, referring to Arizona's Grand Canyon.

Dan Majerle helped them climb back into the series with six 3-pointers as the Suns battled back from an 11-point, fourth-quarter deficit, and finally outlasted the Bulls, 129-121, in triple overtime. The Bulls, however, won Game 4 and were all set to wrap up the title because Game 5 was to be played at Chicago Stadium.

But the Suns wouldn't die quietly. Forward Richard Dumas broke loose for 25 points as the Suns staved off elimination with a 108-98 win in Game 5, sending the series back to Phoenix. The Suns were on the verge of forcing a seventh game, too, but John Paxson's 3-point shot with 3.9 seconds left gave the Bulls a 99-98 victory.

The Suns' other trip to the Finals was equally dramatic. The year was 1976 and the Suns' rise was much more of a surprise. They finished the regular season 42-40, 17 games behind Pacific Division winner Golden State, but played their best basketball in the playoffs.

The Suns upset Seattle in the first round and then shocked the basketball world by eliminating the Warriors in seven games in the Conference Finals. That brought them up against the powerful Boston Celtics, who were seeking their 13th NBA title.

The teams split the first four games, then staged one of the most dramatic Finals games in history. The Suns twice hit clutch baskets to force overtimes before the Celtics finally prevailed, 128-126, in a third overtime. Boston then wrapped up the series in Phoenix.

The two triple-overtime games are the highlights for a franchise that started play in 1968 but only made the playoffs once before its unexpected run in 1976.

PORTLAND BLAZERS

The Portland Trail Blazers started play in the NBA in 1970, but most veteran fans point to 1974 as the team's jumping-off point.

It was in the 1974 Draft that the Blazers claimed a center from UCLA named Bill Walton, who had led the Bruins to two national championships and three Final Fours in three years. Walton played only parts of five seasons with the Blazers due to a series of injuries, but while he was there he was in the middle of the greatest Trail Blazer team in history.

In 1976-77, Walton teamed with Maurice Lucas, Bobby Gross, Dave Twardzik, and Lionel Hollins to take the Blazers to a 49-33 record and their first playoff berth. The team didn't have overwhelming talent but, with Walton manning the post, played brilliant team basketball.

Once they got to the playoffs, the Blazers were, well, blazing. They ousted the Chicago Bulls in three straight games, then upset Midwest Division champion Denver in six. Few gave them a chance against Kareem Abdul-Jabbar and the powerful Lakers, but the Walton Gang was now unstoppable and they blew past L.A. in four straight games.

Waiting for them in the Finals were the powerful Philadelphia 76ers, led by Julius Erving and Darryl Dawkins. Portland dropped the first two games in Philadelphia but then tied the series by scoring 129 and 130 points in two games back home.

In Game 5, the Blazers built a big lead in the third quarter, then held off a 76er rally to win, 110-104. This close to the title, Portland wasn't about to let it slip away. The Blazers had a 12-point lead with 5 minutes left and again had to withstand a 76ers rally. But with the Blazers holding a 109-107 lead with 18 seconds left, Erving and George McGinnis of the Sixers missed shots and the buzzer sounded. The Blazers were champions.

Portland has been back to the Finals twice since then. The 1989-90 team, led by Clyde "The Glide" Drexler and Terry Porter, won 59 regular-season games, then ousted Dallas, San Antonio, and Phoenix to advance to the Finals. But after gaining a split of the first two games in Detroit, the Blazers lost three straight at home and were eliminated. In 1992, Portland won the Pacific Division title and rolled into the Finals, where they were beaten by Michael Jordan and the Bulls in six games.

Rochester. Cincinnati. Kansas City-Omaha. Kansas City. Sacramento. Yes, the Kings have certainly been around in their years in the NBA. And through all their moves there has been one constant: great play from their guards.

Mitch Richmond is the latest in a string of guards who have left their mark on the NBA. Richmond, a 6'5" scorer acquired from Golden State in 1991, averaged better than 21 points per game in each of his first three seasons with the Kings. In 1993-94, he finished seventh in the league in scoring (23.4) and 3-point percentage (.406).

Richmond follows a franchise tradition started by Bob Davies and carried on by Oscar Robertson, Nate Archibald, and Otis Birdsong. Davies was the club's sparkplug in the early days, when the team was based in Rochester and nicknamed the Royals. In 1950-51, he averaged 15.2 points and led the team in assists as the Royals won the only championship in franchise history. The Royals finished second in the Western Division with a 41-27 record, then defeated the Fort Wayne Pistons, Minneapolis Lakers, and New York

Knicks to capture the championship.

The team moved to Cincinnati in 1957 and Robertson came along three years later, after a sensational career at the University of Cincinnati. "The Big O" was a unanimous selection as Rookie of the Year after averaging 30.6 points, 10.1 rebounds, and 9.7 assists, and helping the Royals improve from 19 to 33 wins.

The following season he became the only player in history to average in double figures in points, rebounds, and assists. Robertson and Jerry Lucas combined on some fine teams that might have won championships in the mid-1960s if not for the dominance of the Boston Celtics.

Robertson was traded to Milwaukee in 1970, just in time for Nate "Tiny" Archibald to take over. In 1971-72, the team's first season as the Kansas City-Omaha Kings, Archibald became the first player in history to lead the NBA in scoring and assists. The small, quick Archibald averaged 25.2 points and 8.1 assists in six seasons with the club.

Birdsong joined the team in 1977-78. He spent only four seasons with the Kings but led the club in scoring the last three.

In the nine years since the Kings moved from Kansas City to Sacramento in 1985, they have never finished higher than next-to-last in the Pacific Division. All of the team's major records were made elsewhere. Will Sacramento's time ever come?

Perhaps the miraculous comeback of Bobby Hurley, hurt in a near-fatal auto accident early in the 1993-94 season, will change the tide for the Kings.

The history of the San Antonio Spurs can be divided into two chapters: before David Robinson and after David Robinson. How important is Robinson to the Spurs? Well, consider these arguments: The 1988-89 Spurs had a 21-61 record and were a dreadful 3-38 on the road. The following season, with the rookie Robinson manning the center position, the Spurs finished 56-26. Their 35-game improvement is the largest in NBA history.

Robinson was a unanimous choice as Rookie of the Year in 1990, after averaging 24.3 points, 12 rebounds, and 3.9 blocks. He combined with forwards Terry Cummings and Willie Anderson on a frontline that averaged 61 points per game. The Spurs finished the season with a rush, winning 19 of their last 27 games, then defeated the Denver Nuggets in three straight in the first round of the playoffs. The young Spurs took eventual Western Conference champion Portland into overtime of a seventh game before succumbing.

Robinson and the Spurs have gotten better and better in the 1990s. In the 1993-94 season, the big center won the scoring title with 29.8 points, averaged

10.7 rebounds and 3.31 blocks, and led the Spurs in assists with 4.8 per game. He edged Shaquille O'Neal for the scoring championship by scoring 71 points against the Clippers on the final day of the season.

Robinson was the second Spur to win a scoring title with a last-day barrage. George "Ice" Gervin, one of the NBA's best players in the late 1970s and early 1980s, won scoring honors in 1977-78 by scoring 63 points in the final game of the regular season. He needed almost every one of them because the Nuggets' David Thompson, who would finish second, scored 73 earlier that day. It was the first of three straight scoring titles for Gervin.

The Spurs were one of the old American Basketball Association teams, starting play as the Dallas Chapparals in 1967. They moved to San Antonio in 1973, then joined the Nets, Pacers, and Nuggets as NBA teams three years later. In the first season after the merger, the Spurs played much of the season without their best player, guard James Silas, and still made the playoffs with a 44-38 record.

Once Gervin left after the 1984-85 season, the Spurs struggled until Robinson came along. The 1993-94 Spurs, with Dale Ellis, Dennis Rodman, Vinny Del Negro, and, of course, Robinson showed signs they would be contenders for years to come.

SEATTLE

SEATTLE SUPERSONICS

There was no doubt who was the best team in the NBA in the 1993-94 regular season: it was the Seattle SuperSonics. With superstar forward/center Shawn Kemp and playmaking guard Gary Payton showing the way, the Sonics rolled to a 63-19 record, the best in the league. Included in that record was a 150-point explosion against the Los Angeles Clippers and an amazing 25-5 mark in the tough Pacific Division.

Unfortunately, the Sonics' stretch of success ended in the playoffs. They bolted to a 2-0 lead in their best-of-5 first-round series against the underdog Denver Nuggets and appeared on their way to an easy win. But they lost two games in Denver, giving the Nuggets momentum, and then stunningly lost the decisive fifth game back home in Seattle. The Sonics, who would have had homecourt advantage through the playoffs, saw their magical season end too early.

Once, though, the season did not end too early. It was 1978-79, and the Sonics, under coach Lenny Wilkens, had become an NBA powerhouse. They had made it to the Finals the year before, only to be upset by the Washington Bullets in seven games.

The Sonics had an unusually flexible and cohesive 7-man unit, with John Johnson and Lonnie Shelton at forward, Jack Sikma at center, Dennis Johnson and Gus Williams in the backcourt, and Paul Silas and Fred "Downtown" Brown coming off the bench. They won the Pacific Division title with a 50-32 record and then it was on to the playoffs.

Seattle took out the Lakers in five games and squeezed past the Suns in seven to gain a rematch against the Bullets in the finals. This time, however, the result was different: The Sonics lost the first game, but swept the next four, and Seattle had its championship.

Seattle entered the league as an expansion team in 1967 and suffered through the same growing pains most teams have in their early years. Forward Spencer Haywood, their leading scorer five straight seasons, kept them competitive until the core of the championship team could be built.

© 1994 NBAP

Isiah Thomas, familiar to basketball fans everywhere as a superstar during his 13-year career with the Detroit Pistons, has a new challenge as the vice president of basketball operations with a new NBA team, the Toronto Raptors.

They will begin play in Toronto's SkyDome as the 28th franchise in the NBA in the 1995-96 season. The ownership group is headed by John Bitove, Jr., and includes Allan Sleight, former Ontario premier David Peterson, Philip Granovsky, and the Bank of Nova Scotia.

How in the world did a team with the nickname Jazz end up in Utah? By starting in New Orleans, that's how.

Formed in 1974, the Jazz spent their first five seasons down on the bayou. Their first move was one of the best in team history—the acquisition of superstar guard Pete Maravich, who had starred at Louisiana State and was regarded as a folk hero in the area. But as good as Maravich was (a league-leading 31.1 points per game in 1976-77), the Jazz was unable to surround him with enough talent to make the playoffs.

After failing in their playoff quest, the team moved to Utah in 1979 and decided to keep the nickname Jazz, even though it was not particularly suited to the region where the Mormon faith was born. It took until 1983-84 for the Jazz to make the playoffs, but when they did it, they did it in a big way.

That year the Jazz won the Midwest Division title with a 45-37 record and became the first team in history to have four players win individual titles. Forward Adrian Dantley won the scoring championship

(30.6), center Mark Eaton led in blocks (4.28), guard Darrell Griffith was the 3-point percentage leader (.361), and guard Rickey Green was tops in steals (2.65). The Jazz won their first-ever playoff series, defeating the Nuggets in five games before losing to the Suns in a 6-game conference semifinal series.

The Jazz of the 1990s always seemed to be on the verge of greatness but failed to take the step that would put them in the Finals.

The 1991-92 team was perhaps the best in franchise history, winning the Midwest Division championship with a 55-27 record. With John Stockton running the show (a league-best 13.7 assists per game) and forward Karl Malone providing scoring (28.0) and rebounding (11.2), the Jazz roared into the playoffs.

They defeated the Clippers and then wiped out the SuperSonics in five games to advance to the Western Conference Finals against Portland. But after climbing back from a 2-game deficit to tie the series, the Jazz lost a pivotal fifth game in overtime in Portland. The Blazers then closed out the series with a victory in Utah in Game 6.

The Jazz had no playoff success in 1992-93, losing a 5-game series to Seattle, but they won two rounds in 1993-94 before losing to the eventual champion Houston Rockets in the Conference Finals.

Hockey may be the national sport of Canada, but there'll be a new game in Vancouver—pro basketball—in the 1995-96 season when the Vancouver Grizzlies make their debut in the NBA.

A group headed by Arthur Griffith, owner of the National Hockey League's Vancouver Canucks, was granted the NBA's 29th franchise and will be joined by another Canadian team, the Toronto Raptors.

Stu Jackson, who was head coach of the New York Knicks before he coached at the University of Wisconsin, is vice president and general manager of the team. The Grizzlies' home arena will be GM Place.

"The opera isn't over till the fat lady sings." That's the motto that sparked the Washington Bullets to their greatest moment of glory—the 1978 NBA championship.

Ironically, this was a year the Bullets were given little chance to win a title. It was the 1974-75 team that was supposed to win; that team coasted to the Central Division title with a 60-22 record. Elvin Hayes, a 6'9" smooth-shooting forward, was at the peak of his game, averaging 23 points and finishing eighth in rebounds and fourth in blocks.

With Wes Unseld rebounding and setting picks, and league assist leader Kevin Porter running the offense, the Bullets were odds-on favorites to capture their first title. But after defeating Buffalo in seven games and Boston in six, the Bullets ran into a roadblock in the Finals, with the Golden State Warriors stunning them four straight times to take the championship.

The 1977-78 team gave little hint of what was to come. Hayes and Unseld were still there, and the addition of forward Bob Dandridge gave the Bullets another scoring threat. But the Bullets finished the regular season with only 44 wins, tied for eighth in the overall standings, and thoughts of a championship seemed pretty far-fetched.

Even after playoff wins over Atlanta, San Antonio, and Philadelphia, the Bullets' task appeared too tough. They fell behind the Seattle SuperSonics two games to one and had to play the next two games in Seattle. When asked if it was over, the Bullets responded with their battle cry, "It ain't over till the fat lady sings."

They were right. The Bullets won Game 4 in overtime to earn the split they needed in Seattle. Then, down 3-2, they trounced the Sonics, 117-82, back at home and then won again, 105-99, in Seattle to bring the title back to Washington. It was the last time any team won Game 7 of the Finals on the road.

The birth of the Bullets actually was in Chicago, back in 1961. The expansion Chicago Packers (who later changed their nickname to Zephyrs) spent their early years in the Windy City before moving to Baltimore and becoming the Bullets in 1963. They became known as the Capital Bullets in 1974 before becoming the Washington Bullets the following year.

The Bullets of the 1990s were rebuilding behind forwards Tom Gugliotta (now with Golden State) and Don MacLean and guard Calbert Cheaney. And they were looking for big things from Juwan Howard, the 6'8" forward from Michigan who was the No. 5 pick overall in the 1994 Draft, and forward-center Chris Webber. Webber joined the team in a November 1994 trade for Gugliotta and three future first-round draft picks.

The Basketball Hall of Fame

He started it all in Springfield, Massachusetts, with a peach basket. That was more than 100 years ago, in 1891, when Dr. James Naismith invented the game of basketball.

Not far from the original site in Springfield is the Basketball Hall of Fame.

It is a modern, 3-level structure on the banks of the Connecticut River and it has something for basketball fans from 8 to 80.

Here are housed the sport's immortals from every level—professional, college, high school, amateur, and the Olympics—with photos, memorabilia, and movies covering the history of the game. And there's even an exhibit that enables visitors to play one-on-one—via advanced video technology—against Hall-of-Famer Bill Walton. There's also a "Shoot-Out" in which fans on a moving sidewalk get a chance to shoot baskets at different heights and from varying distances.

As for the honored inductees in the Hall, nominations are made in four categories—player, coach, referee, and contributor. The Honors committee, composed of 24 members representing all levels of basketball, votes each year on the nominees. Eighteen votes are required for election. Players have to be retired for five years before they are eligible.

Hall of Fame Electees

Individuals associated with NBA appear in bold type.
*Deceased

PLAYERS

Name	Year Elected
Archibald, Nate	**1991**
Arizin, Paul	**1977**
* Barlow, Thomas "Tarzan"	1980
Barry, Rick	**1986**
Baylor, Elgin	**1976**
* Beckman, John	1973
Bellamy, Walt	**1993**
Belov, Sergei	1992
Bing, Dave	**1990**
Blazejowski, Carol	**1994**
Bradley, Bill	**1982**
* Brennan, Joe	1974
Cervi, Al	**1984**
Chamberlain, Wilt	**1978**
* Cooper, Charles "Tarzan"	1967
Cousy, Bob	**1970**
Cowens, Dave	**1991**
Cuningham, Billy	**1985**
* **Davies, Bob**	**1969**
* DeBernardi, Forrest "Red"	1961
DeBusschere, Dave	**1982**
* Dehnert, Henry "Dutch"	1968
Endacott, Paul	1971
Erving, Julius	**1993**
Foster, Harold "Bud"	1964
Frazier, Walt "Clyde"	**1986**
* Friedman, Max "Marty"	1971
* **Fulks, Joe**	**1977**
Gale, Lauren "Laddie"	1976
Gallatin, Harry	**1991**
Gates, William "Pop"	1988
Gola, Tom	**1975**
Greer, Hal	**1981**
* Gruenig, Robert "Ace"	1963
Hagan, Cliff	**1977**
* Hanson, Victor	1960
Havlicek, John	**1983**
Hawkins, Connie	**1992**
Hayes, Elvin	**1990**
Heinsohn, Tom	**1985**
Holman, Nat	1964
Houbregs, Robert	**1986**
* Hyatt, Charles "Chuck"	1959
Issel, Dan	**1993**
Jeannette, Harry	**1994**
Johnson, William	1976
* **Johnston, Neil**	**1990**
Jones, K.C.	**1988**
Jones, Sam	**1983**
* Krause, Edward "Moose"	1975
Kurland, Bob	1961
Lanier, Bob	**1992**
* **Lapchick, Joe**	**1966**
Lovellette, Clyde	**1987**
Lucas, Jerry	**1979**
Luisetti, Angelo "Hank"	1959

Macauley, Edward "Easy Ed"	**1960**
***Maravich, Pete**	**1986**
Martin, Slater	**1981**
* McCracken, Branch	1960
* McCracken, Jack	1962
McDermott, Bobby	1987
McGuire, Dick	**1993**
Meyers, Ann	1993
Mikan, George	**1959**
Monroe, Earl	**1990**
Murphy, Calvin	**1993**
* Murphy, Charles "Stretch"	1960
* Page, Harlan "Pat"	1962
Pettit, Bob	**1970**
Phillip, Andy	**1961**
***Pollard, Jim**	**1977**
Ramsey, Frank	**1981**
Reed, Willis	**1981**
Robertson, Oscar	**1979**
* Roosma, John	1961
Russell, Bill	**1974**
***Russell, John "Honey"**	**1964**
Schayes, Dolph	**1972**
* Schmidt, Ernest	1973
* Schommer, John	1959
* Sedran, Barney	1962
Semjonova, Uljana	1993
Sharman, Bill	**1975**
* Steinmetz, Christian	1961
Harris-Stewart, Lusia	1992
* Thompson, John "Cat"	1962
Thurmond, Nate	**1984**
Twyman, Jack	**1982**
Unseld, Wes	**1987**
Vandiver, Robert "Fuzzy"	1974

* Wachter, Edward	1961
Walton, Bill	**1993**
Wanzer, Bobby	**1986**
West, Jerry	**1979**
White, Nera	1992
Wilkens, Lenny	**1988**
Wooden, John	1960

Coaches

Name	Year Elected
Anderson, Harold	1984
Auerbach, Arnold "Red"	**1968**
* Barry, Justin "Sam"	1978
* Blood, Ernest	1960
* Cann, Howard "Jake"	1965
* Carlson, Dr. H. Clifford	1959
Carnesecca, Lou	1992
Carnevale, Ben	1969
* Case, Everett	1981
Crum, Denny	1994
Daly, Chuck	**1994**
* Dean, Everett	1966
* Diddle, Ed	1971
* Drake, Bruce	1972
Gaines, Clarence	1981
Gardner, Jack	1983
* Gill, Amory "Slats"	1967
Harshman, Marv	1984
* Hickey, Ed	1978
* Hobson, Howard	1965
Holzman, William "Red"	**1985**
* Iba, Henry "Hank"	1968
***Julian, Alvin "Doggie"**	**1967**
* Keaney, Frank	1960
* Keogan, George	1961

Knight, Bobby	1991
* Lambert, Ward "Piggy"	1960
Litwack, Harry	1975
* Loeffler, Ken	1964
* Lonborg, Arthur "Dutch"	1972
* McCutchan, Arad	1980
McGuire, Al	**1992**
McGuire, Frank	**1976**
* Meanwell, Dr. Walter	1959
Meyer, Ray	1978
Miller, Ralph	1987
Ramsay, Jack	1992
Rubini, Cesare	1994
* Rupp, Adolph	1968
* Sachs, Leonard	1961
* Shelton, Everett	1979
Smith, Dean	1982
Taylor, Fred	1985
Wade, Margaret	1984
Watts, Stanley	1985
Wooden, John	1972
* Woolpert, Phil	1992

Contributors

* Abbot, Senda Berenson	1984
* Allen, Dr. Forrest "Phog"	1959
Bee, Clair	**1967**
Brown, Walter	**1965**
* Bunn, John	1964
* Douglas, Robert	1971
* Duer, Alva	1981
Fagan, Clifford	1983
* Fisher, Harry	1973
Fleisher, Lawrence	**1991**
Gottlieb, Eddie	**1971**

* Gulick, Dr. Luther	1959
Harrison, Lester	**1979**
* Hepp, Ferenc	1980
* Hickox, Edward	1959
* Hinkle, Paul "Tony"	1965
Irish, Ned	**1964**
* Jones, R. William	1964
Kennedy, Walter	**1980**
* Liston, Emil	1974
McLendon, John	1978
Mokray, Bill	**1965**
* Morgan, Ralph	1959
* Morgenweck, Frank	1962
* Naismith, Dr. James	1959
Newell, Pete	**1978**
* O'Brien, John	1961
O'Brien, Lawrence	**1991**
Olsen, Harold	**1959**
Podoloff, Maurice	**1973**
* Porter, Henry	1960
* Reid, William	1963
* Ripley, Elmer	1972
* St. John, Lynn	1962
* Saperstein, Abe	1970
* Schabinger, Arthur	1961
* Stagg, Amos Alonzo	1959
Stankovic, Boris	1991
* Steitz, Edward	1983
* Taylor, Charles "Chuck"	1968
* Teague, Bertha	1984
* Tower, Oswald	1959
* Trester, Arthur	1961
* Wells, Clifford	1971
* Wilke, Lou	1982

Referees

| **Enright, Jim** | **1978** |
| Hepbron, George | 1960 |

* Hoyt, George	1961
* Kennedy, Matthew "Pat"	**1959**
* Leith, Lloyd	1982
Mihalik, Zig "Red"	1985
Nucatola, John	**1977**
* Quigley, Ernest	1961
* Shirley, J. Dallas	**1979**
* Tobey, David	1961
* Walsh, David	1961

Teams

First Team	1959
Original Celtics	1959
Buffalo Germans	1961
New York Renaissance	1963

212

Be a Super Stat Star

— ■ ■ ■ —

The drama is on the court, but basketball fans know there's always a story in the statistics. The daily newspapers provide the basics in box scores, standings, averages, and individual leaders. But some followers of the sport enjoy doing their own stats. Here's how you do it.

Scoring

To get a scoring average, take the player's total points and divide them by the number of games played. For example, if Penny Hardaway has scored 91 points in his first 7 games, divide 91 by 7, which comes to 13 points per game.

QUICK QUIZ

1. Shaquille O'Neal has scored 36, 27, and 32 points in his first three games. What is O'Neal's scoring average?

2. David Robinson scored 123 points in his first five games and then had back-to-back 40-point games. What is Robinson's average?

3. Hakeem Olajuwon scored 175 points in the first six games of a playoff series. How many points will he need to score in Game 7 to average 30 points in the series?

See answers on page 217.

Shooting Percentage

To figure out a shooting percentage, take the player's shots made and divide them by the number of shots attempted. For example, if Shawn Kemp has made 9 of 15 shots, you divide 9 by 15, which is .600, or 60 percent.

QUICK QUIZ

1. On a 3-game road trip, Chris Webber shot 4-for-9, 10-for-16, and 8-for-14. What is Webber's shooting percentage?

2. If Alonzo Mourning makes his first nine free throws and then misses one, what is his free-throw percentage?

3. If Reggie Miller connects on 5 of 11 3-pointers one night and 4 of 9 the next, what is his 3-point shooting percentage?

See answers on page 217.

Rebounding

To figure out a rebounding average, take the player's total rebounds and divide them by the number of games played. For example, if Patrick Ewing has grabbed 46 rebounds in five games, you divide 46 by 5, which is 9.2 rebounds per game.

QUICK QUIZ

1. If Dennis Rodman grabs 15, 17, 12, 20, and 16 rebounds in a 5-game stretch, what is his rebounding average?

2. If Charles Oakley has 37 rebounds in four games,

how many rebounds does he need in his next game to average exactly 10?

3. Who has a higher rebound average: Horace Grant with 65 rebounds in seven games, or Karl Malone with 72 rebounds in eight games?

See answers on page 217.

Assists

To figure out a player's assist average, take his total assists and divide them by the number of games played. For example, if Tim Hardaway has 84 assists in 12 games, you divide 84 by 12, which is 7.0 assists per game.

QUICK QUIZ

1. If John Stockton is credited with 11, 8, 12, and 13 assists in a 4-game stretch, what is his assist average?

2. If Mark Jackson has 42 assists in four games, how many assists does he need in his next game to average exactly 11?

3. Who has a higher assist average, Muggsy Bogues with 39 assists in five games, or Mookie Blaylock with 33 assists in four games?

See answers on page 217.

Blocked Shots

To figure out a player's blocked-shot average, take his total blocks and divide them by the number of games played. For example, if Shawn Bradley has 27 blocks in 12 games, you divide 27 by 12, which is 2.25 blocks per game.

QUICK QUIZ

1. If Dikembe Mutombo has 22 blocks in four games, how many blocks does he need in his next game to average exactly six?

2. If Alonzo Mourning is credited with five, three, seven, and five blocks in a 4-game stretch, what is his blocked-shot average?

3. Who has a higher blocked-shot average, David Robinson with 41 blocks in 11 games, or Hakeem Olajuwon with 36 blocks in 10 games?

See answers on page 217.

Steals

To figure out a player's average number of steals, take his total steals and divide them by the number of games played. For example, if Eric Murdock has 36 steals in 15 games, you divide 36 by 15, which is 2.40 steals per game.

QUICK QUIZ

1. If Scottie Pippen has 35 steals in 12 games, how many steals does he need in his next game to average exactly three?

2. If Gary Payton is credited with three, three, five, and two steals in a 4-game stretch, what is his steals average?

3. Who has a higher steals average, Latrell Sprewell with 23 steals in 9 games, or Mookie Blaylock with 27 steals in 12 games?

See answers on bottom of page.

ANSWERS TO QUICK QUIZZES

Scoring Average: 1. 31.67 2. 29.0 3. 35
Shooting Percentage: 1. 56.4 2. 90.0 3. 45.0
Rebounding: 1. 16 2. 13 3. Grant 9.3, Malone 9.0
Assists: 1. 11.0 2. 13 3. Blaylock 8.25, Bogues 7.8
Blocked Shots: 1. 8 2. 5.0 3. Robinson 3.7, Olajuwon 3.6
Steals: 1. 4 2. 3.25 3. Sprewell 2.55, Blaylock 2.25

NBA Champions and Award Winners

No team has ever won as many NBA titles as the Boston Celtics. They have reached the winners' circle 16 times, including 8 in a row in the 1950s and 1960s. The runner-up Los Angeles Lakers have taken the crown six times and, adding their earlier years as a franchise in Minneapolis, the Lakers total 11 championships.

NBA CHAMPIONS

Season	Champion	Eastern Division W.	L.		Western Division W.	L.	
1946-47	Philadelphia	49	11	Washington	39	22	Chicago
1947-48	Baltimore	27	21	Philadelphia	29	19	St. Louis
1948-49	Minneapolis	38	22	Washington	45	15	Rochester
1949-50	Minneapolis	51	13	Syracuse	39	25	Indianapolis*
1950-51	Rochester	36	30	New York	44	24	Minneapolis
1951-52	Minneapolis	37	29	New York	41	25	Rochester
1952-53	Minneapolis	47	23	New York	48	22	Minneapolis
1953-54	Minneapolis	42	30	Syracuse	46	26	Minneapolis
1954-55	Syracuse	43	29	Syracuse	43	29	Ft. Wayne
1955-56	Philadelphia	45	27	Philadelphia	37	35	Ft. Wayne
1956-57	Boston	44	28	Boston	34	38	StL-Mpl-FtW
1957-58	St. Louis	49	23	Boston	41	31	St. Louis
1958-59	Boston	52	20	Boston	49	23	St. Louis
1959-60	Boston	59	16	Boston	46	29	St. Louis
1960-61	Boston	57	22	Boston	51	28	St. Louis
1961-62	Boston	60	20	Boston	54	26	Los Angeles
1962-63	Boston	58	22	Boston	53	27	Los Angeles
1963-64	Boston	59	21	Boston	48	32	San Francisco
1964-65	Boston	62	18	Boston	49	31	Los Angeles
1965-66	Boston	54	26	Boston	45	35	Los Angeles
1966-67	Philadelphia	68	13	Philadelphia	44	37	San Francisco
1967-68	Boston	54	28	Boston	52	30	Los Angeles
1968-69	Boston	48	34	Boston	55	27	Los Angeles
1969-70	New York	60	22	New York	46	36	Los Angeles
1970-71	Milwaukee	42	40	Baltimore	66	16	Milwaukee
1971-72	Los Angeles	48	34	New York	69	13	Los Angeles
1972-73	New York	57	25	New York	60	22	Los Angeles
1973-74	Boston	56	26	Boston	59	23	Milwaukee
1974-75	Golden State	60	22	Washington	48	34	Golden State
1975-76	Boston	54	28	Boston	42	40	Phoenix
1976-77	Portland	50	32	Philadelphia	49	33	Portland
1977-78	Washington	44	38	Washington	47	35	Seattle
1978-79	Seattle	54	28	Washington	52	30	Seattle
1979-80	Los Angeles	59	23	Philadelphia	60	22	Los Angeles
1980-81	Boston	62	20	Boston	40	42	Houston
1981-82	Los Angeles	58	24	Philadelphia	57	25	Los Angeles
1982-83	Philadelphia	65	17	Philadelphia	58	24	Los Angeles
1983-84	Boston	62	20	Boston	54	28	Los Angeles
1984-85	L.A. Lakers	63	19	Boston	62	20	L.A. Lakers
1985-86	Boston	67	15	Boston	51	31	Houston
1986-87	L.A. Lakers	59	23	Boston	65	17	L.A. Lakers
1987-88	L.A. Lakers	54	28	Detroit	62	20	L.A. Lakers
1988-89	Detroit	63	19	Detroit	57	25	L.A. Lakers
1989-90	Detroit	59	23	Detroit	59	23	Portland

1990-91	Chicago	61	21	Chicago	58	24	L.A. Lakers
1991-92	Chicago	67	15	Chicago	57	25	Portland
1992-93	Chicago	57	25	Chicago	62	20	Phoenix
1993-94	Houston	57	25	New York	58	24	Houston

*1949-50 Central Division Champion: Minneapolis and Rochester tied 51-17.

NBA Scoring Champions

Wilt Chamberlain and Michael Jordan share honors for most scoring titles (7). Wilt did it with the Philadelphia and San Francisco Warriors and Philadelphia 76ers. Jordan's came as the leader of the three-time champion Chicago Bulls.

NBA SCORING CHAMPIONS

Season	Pts./Avg.	Top Scorer	Team
1946-47	1389	Joe Fulks	Philadelphia
1947-48	1007	Max Zaslofsky	Chicago
1948-49	1698	George Mikan	Minneapolis
1949-50	1865	George Mikan	Minneapolis
1950-51	1932	George Mikan	Minneapolis
1951-52	1674	Paul Arizin	Philadelphia
1952-53	1564	Neil Johnston	Philadelphia
1953-54	1759	Neil Johnston	Philadelphia
1954-55	1631	Neil Johnston	Philadelphia
1955-56	1849	Bob Pettit	St. Louis
1956-57	1817	Paul Arizin	Philadelphia
1957-58	2001	George Yardley	Detroit
1958-59	2105	Bob Pettit	St. Louis
1959-60	2707	Wilt Chamberlain	Philadelphia
1960-61	3033	Wilt Chamberlain	Philadelphia
1961-62	4029	Wilt Chamberlain	Philadelphia
1962-63	3586	Wilt Chamberlain	San Francisco
1963-64	2948	Wilt Chamberlain	San Francisco
1964-65	2534	Wilt Chamberlain	San Francisco-Philadelphia
1965-66	2649	Wilt Chamberlain	Philadelphia
1966-67	2775	Rick Barry	San Francisco

1967-68	2142	Dave Bing	Detroit
1968-69	2327	Elvin Hayes	San Diego
1969-70	*31.2	Jerry West	Los Angeles
1970-71	*31.7	K. Abdul-Jabbar	Milwaukee
1971-72	*34.8	K. Abdul-Jabbar	Milwaukee
1972-73	*34.0	Nate Archibald	K.C.-Omaha
1973-74	*30.6	Bob McAdoo	Buffalo
1974-75	*34.5	Bob McAdoo	Buffalo
1975-76	*31.1	Bob McAdoo	Buffalo
1976-77	*31.1	Pete Maravich	New Orleans
1977-78	*27.2	George Gervin	San Antonio
1978-79	*29.6	George Gervin	San Antonio
1979-80	*33.1	George Gervin	San Antonio
1980-81	*30.7	Adrian Dantley	Utah
1981-82	*32.3	George Gervin	San Antonio
1982-83	*28.4	Alex English	Denver
1983-84	*30.6	Adrian Dantley	Utah
1984-85	*32.9	Bernard King	New York
1985-86	*30.3	Dominique Wilkins	Atlanta
1986-87	*37.1	Michael Jordan	Chicago
1987-88	*35.0	Michael Jordan	Chicago
1988-89	*32.5	Michael Jordan	Chicago
1989-90	*33.6	Michael Jordan	Chicago
1990-91	*31.2	Michael Jordan	Chicago
1991-92	*30.1	Michael Jordan	Chicago
1992-93	*32.6	Michael Jordan	Chicago
1993-94	*29.8	David Robinson	San Antonio

*Scoring title based on best average with at least 70 games played or 1,400 points

FINALS MVP AWARD

1969	Jerry West, Los Angeles
1970	Willis Reed, New York
1971	Kareem Abdul-Jabbar, Milwaukee
1972	Wilt Chamberlain, Los Angeles
1973	Willis Reed, New York
1974	John Havlicek, Boston
1975	Rick Barry, Golden State
1976	Jo Jo White, Boston
1977	Bill Walton, Portland
1978	Wes Unseld, Washington
1979	Dennis Johnson, Seattle
1980	Magic Johnson, Los Angeles
1981	Cedric Maxwell, Boston

1982	Magic Johnson, Los Angeles
1983	Moses Malone, Philadelphia
1984	Larry Bird, Boston
1985	Kareem Abdul-Jabbar, L.A. Lakers
1986	Larry Bird, Boston
1987	Magic Johnson, L.A. Lakers
1988	James Worthy, L.A. Lakers
1989	Joe Dumars, Detroit
1990	Isiah Thomas, Detroit
1991	Michael Jordan, Chicago
1992	Michael Jordan, Chicago
1993	Michael Jordan, Chicago
1994	Hakeem Olajuwon, Houston

DEFENSIVE PLAYER OF THE YEAR

1982-83 Sidney Moncrief, Milwaukee	1988-89 Mark Eaton, Utah
1983-84 Sidney Moncrief, Milwaukee	1989-90 Dennis Rodman, Detroit
1984-85 Mark Eaton, Utah	1990-91 Dennis Rodman, Detroit
1985-86 Alvin Robertson, San Antonio	1991-92 David Robinson, San Antonio
1986-87 Michael Cooper, L.A. Lakers	1992-93 Hakeem Olajuwon, Houston
1987-88 Michael Jordan, Chicago	1993-94 Hakeem Olajuwon, Houston

SIXTH MAN AWARD

1982-83 Bobby Jones, Philadelphia	1988-89 Eddie Johnson, Phoenix
1983-84 Kevin McHale, Boston	1989-90 Ricky Pierce, Milwaukee
1984-85 Kevin McHale, Boston	1990-91 Detlef Schrempf, Indiana
1985-86 Bill Walton, Boston	1991-92 Detlef Schrempf, Indiana
1986-87 Ricky Pierce, Milwaukee	1992-93 Cliff Robinson, Portland
1987-88 Roy Tarpley, Dallas	1993-94 Dell Curry, Charlotte

MOST IMPROVED PLAYER

1985-86 Alvin Robertson, San Antonio	1990-91 Scott Skiles, Orlando
1986-87 Dale Ellis, Seattle	1991-92 Pervis Ellison, Washington
1987-88 Kevin Duckworth, Portland	1992-93 Chris Jackson, Denver
1988-89 Kevin Johnson, Phoenix	1993-94 Don MacLean, Washington
1989-90 Rony Seikaly, Miami	

IBM AWARD
Determined by Computer Formula

1983-84 Magic Johnson, Los Angeles	1989-90 David Robinson, San Antonio
1984-85 Michael Jordan, Chicago	1990-91 David Robinson, San Antonio
1985-86 Charles Barkley, Philadelphia	1991-92 Dennis Rodman, Detroit
1986-87 Charles Barkley, Philadelphia	1992-93 Hakeem Olajuwon, Houston
1987-88 Charles Barkley, Philadelphia	1993-94 David Robinson, San Antonio
1988-89 Michael Jordan, Chicago	

COACH OF THE YEAR

1962-63 Harry Gallatin, St. Louis	1970-71 Dick Motta, Chicago
1963-64 Alex Hannum, San Francisco	1971-72 Bill Sharman, Los Angeles
1964-65 Red Auerbach, Boston	1972-73 Tom Heinsohn, Boston
1965-66 Dolph Schayes, Philadelphia	1973-74 Ray Scott, Detroit
1966-67 Johnny Kerr, Chicago	1974-75 Phil Johnson, Kansas City-Omaha
1967-68 Richie Guerin, St. Louis	1975-76 Bill Fitch, Cleveland
1968-69 Gene Shue, Baltimore	1976-77 Tom Nissalke, Houston
1969-70 Red Holzman, New York	1977-78 Hubie Brown, Atlanta

1978-79	Cotton Fitzsimmons, Kansas City	1986-87	Mike Schuler, Portland
1979-80	Bill Fitch, Boston	1987-88	Doug Moe, Denver
1980-81	Jack McKinney, Indiana	1988-89	Cotton Fitzsimmons, Phoenix
1981-82	Gene Shue, Washington		
1982-83	Don Nelson, Milwaukee	1989-90	Pat Riley, L.A. Lakers
1983-84	Frank Layden, Utah	1990-91	Don Chaney, Houston
1984-85	Don Nelson, Milwaukee	1991-92	Don Nelson, Golden State
1985-86	Mike Fratello, Atlanta	1992-93	Pat Riley, New York
		1993-94	Lenny Wilkens, Atlanta

J. WALTER KENNEDY CITIZENSHIP AWARD

1974-75	Wes Unseld, Washington	1985-86	Michael Cooper, L.A. Lakers
1975-76	Slick Watts, Seattle		Rory Sparrow, New York
1976-77	Dave Bing, Washington	1986-87	Isiah Thomas, Detroit
1977-78	Bob Lanier, Detroit	1987-88	Alex English, Denver
1978-79	Calvin Murphy, Houston	1988-89	Thurl Bailey, Utah
1979-80	Austin Carr, Cleveland	1989-90	Glenn Rivers, Atlanta
1980-81	Mike Glenn, New York	1990-91	Kevin Johnson, Phoenix
1981-82	Kent Benson, Detroit	1991-92	Magic Johnson, L.A. Lakers
1982-83	Julius Erving, Philadelphia	1992-93	Terry Porter, Portland
1983-84	Frank Layden, Utah	1993-94	Joe Dumars, Detroit
1984-85	Dan Issel, Denver		

MOST VALUABLE PLAYER

1955-56	Bob Pettit, St. Louis	1975-76	Kareem Abdul-Jabbar, L.A.
1956-57	Bob Cousy, Boston	1976-77	Kareem Abdul-Jabbar, L.A.
1957-58	Bill Russell, Boston	1977-78	Bill Walton, Portland
1958-59	Bob Pettit, St. Louis	1978-79	Moses Malone, Houston
1959-60	Wilt Chamberlain, Philadelphia	1979-80	Kareem Abdul-Jabbar, L.A.
1960-61	Bill Russell, Boston	1980-81	Julius Erving, Philadelphia
1961-62	Bill Russell, Boston	1981-82	Moses Malone, Houston
1962-63	Bill Russell, Boston	1982-83	Moses Malone, Philadelphia
1963-64	Oscar Robertson, Cincinnati	1983-84	Larry Bird, Boston
1964-65	Bill Russell, Boston	1984-85	Larry Bird, Boston
1965-66	Wilt Chamberlain, Philadelphia	1985-86	Larry Bird, Boston
1966-67	Wilt Chamberlain, Philadelphia	1986-87	Magic Johnson, L.A. Lakers
1967-68	Wilt Chamberlain, Philadelphia	1987-88	Michael Jordan, Chicago
1968-69	Wes Unseld, Baltimore	1988-89	Magic Johnson, L.A. Lakers
1969-70	Willis Reed, New York	1989-90	Magic Johnson, L.A. Lakers
1970-71	Kareem Abdul-Jabbar, Milwaukee	1990-91	Michael Jordan, Chicago
1971-72	Kareem Abdul-Jabbar, Milwaukee	1991-92	Michael Jordan, Chicago
1972-73	Dave Cowens	1992-93	Charles Barkley, Phoenix
1973-74	Kareem Abdul-Jabbar, Milwaukee	1993-94	Hakeem Olajuwon, Houston
1974-75	Bob McAdoo, Buffalo		

ROOKIE OF THE YEAR

1947-48	Paul Hoffman, Baltimore
1948-49	Howie Shannon, Providence
1949-50	Alex Groza, Indianapolis
1950-51	Paul Arizin, Philadelphia
1951-52	Bill Tosheff, Indianapolis
	Mel Hutchins, Milwaukee
1952-53	Don Meineke, Fort Wayne
1953-54	Ray Felix, Baltimore
1954-55	Bob Pettit, Milwaukee
1955-56	Maurice Stokes, Rochester
1956-57	Tom Heinsohn, Boston
1957-58	Woody Sauldsberry, Philadelphia
1958-59	Elgin Baylor, Minneapolis
1959-60	Wilt Chamberlain, Philadelphia
1960-61	Oscar Robertson, Cincinnati
1961-62	Walt Bellamy, Chicago
1962-63	Terry Dischinger, Chicago
1963-64	Jerry Lucas, Cincinnati
1964-65	Willis Reed, New York
1965-66	Rick Barry, San Francisco
1966-67	Dave Bing, Detroit
1967-68	Earl Monroe, Baltimore
1968-69	Wes Unseld, Baltimore
1969-70	Kareem Abdul-Jabbar, Milwaukee
1970-71	Dave Cowens, Boston
	Geoff Petrie, Portland
1971-72	Sidney Wicks, Portland
1972-73	Bob McAdoo, Buffalo
1973-74	Ernie DiGregorio, Buffalo
1974-75	Keith Wilkes, Golden State.
1976-77	Adrian Dantley, Buffalo
1977-78	Walter Davis, Phoenix
1978-79	Phil Ford, Kansas City
1979-80	Larry Bird, Boston
1980-81	Darrell Griffith, Utah
1981-82	Buck Williams, New Jersey
1982-83	Terry Cummings, San Diego
1983-84	Ralph Sampson, Houston
1984-85	Michael Jordan, Chicago
1985-86	Patrick Ewing, New York
1986-87	Chuck Person, Indiana
1987-88	Mark Jackson, New York
1988-89	Mitch Richmond, Golden State
1989-90	David Robinson, San Antonio
1990-91	Derrick Coleman, New Jersey
1991-92	Larry Johnson, Charlotte
1992-93	Shaquille O'Neal, Orlando
1993-94	Chris Webber, Golden State

The NBA Record Book

— — —

Some NBA records will live forever. Others are in danger of being broken this season and in the future. Here's a look at some super stats, amazing achievements, NBA Top 10s, and records that have made sports history.

Most Games Played

He started his career with Richard Nixon as president and ended it with George Bush. In the long history of the NBA, no one has played more games than Kareem Abdul-Jabbar, who came into the league as Lew Alcindor in 1969 and proceeded to rewrite the NBA record book.

The main challenge to Abdul-Jabbar has come from Robert Parish, who at the age of 41 was starting his 18th NBA season in 1994-95.

Kareem Abdul-Jabbar	1,560
Robert Parish	1,413
Moses Malone	1,312
Elvin Hayes	1,303
John Havlicek	1,270
Paul Silas	1,254
Alex English	1,193
Hal Greer	1,122
Jack Sikma	1,107
Maurice Cheeks	1,101

Most Points

Can anyone ever overtake Kareem Abdul-Jabbar and become the league's all-time scorer? It looked like Michael Jordan might do it, but the ex-Bulls' superstar gave up basketball to pursue a baseball career in 1994. Dominique Wilkins vaulted into the Top 10 in 1993-94 and was poised to move past several more of the NBA's all-time greats in 1994-95.

David Robinson and Shaquille O'Neal, who battled for the scoring title in 1994, are perhaps the best bets to someday challenge the leaders.

Kareem Abdul-Jabbar	38,387
Wilt Chamberlain	31,419
Moses Malone	27,360
Elvin Hayes	27,313
Oscar Robertson	26,710
John Havlicek	26,395
Alex English	25,613
Jerry West	25,192
Dominique Wilkins	24,019
Adrian Dantley	23,177

Most Points in a Game

Only one active player, San Antonio's David Robinson, is in the Top 10 single-game scorers. In addition to making him scoring champion for the 1993-94 season, Robinson's 71 points in the final game of the regular season vaulted him into the Top 10, but were nowhere near Philadelphia and San Francisco's Wilt Chamberlain, who tops them all with 100. Wilt dominates the list, having scored 70 or more points six times.

Wilt Chamberlain	100	Philadelphia vs. New York, March 2, 1962
Wilt Chamberlain	78	Philadelphia vs. Los Angeles (3 OT), Dec. 8, 1961
Wilt Chamberlain	73	Philadelphia vs. Chicago, Jan. 13, 1962
Wilt Chamberlain	73	San Francisco vs. New York, Nov. 16, 1962
David Thompson	73	Denver vs. Detroit, April 9, 1978
Wilt Chamberlain	72	San Francisco vs. Los Angeles, Nov. 3, 1962
Elgin Baylor	71	Los Angeles vs. New York, Nov. 15, 1960
David Robinson	71	San Antonio vs. L.A. Clippers, April 24, 1994
Wilt Chamberlain	70	San Francisco vs. Syracuse, March 10, 1963
Michael Jordan	69	Chicago vs. Cleveland, March 28, 1990

Highest Scoring Average
(Minimum 400 Games or 10,000 Points)

Michael Jordan's nickname was "Air," but it might as well have been "Rare." Rarely has a player come into the NBA and dominated it the way Jordan did in the late 1980s and early 1990s. Jordan tied Wilt Chamberlain's record of seven straight scoring championships and finished his career with a record 32.3 average, more than two points higher than "The Big Dipper."

David Robinson is on the verge of cracking the Top 10 but was six games short of the 400-game minimum entering the 1994-95 season. In 394 career games, Robinson had scored 9.971 points, an average of 25.3 per game.

	Games	Points	Average
Michael Jordan	667	21,541	32.3
Wilt Chamberlain	1,045	31,419	30.1
Elgin Baylor	846	23,149	27.4
Jerry West	932	25,192	27.0
Dominique Wilkins	907	24,019	26.5
Bob Pettit	792	20,880	26.4
George Gervin	791	20,708	26.2
Karl Malone	734	19,050	26.0
Oscar Robertson	1,040	26,710	25.7
Kareem Abdul-Jabbar	1,560	38,387	24.6

Most Field Goals Made

It's a basic play in Orlando. Penny Hardaway brings the ball downcourt, finds Shaquille O'Neal on the low post, and Shaq overpowers his defender for a dunk. The play was so effective that in 1993-94 O'Neal led the NBA with 953 field goals, 59 more than any other player.

Shaq would have to average 900 field goals for more than 17 seasons to catch Kareem Abdul-Jabbar, who set an almost unreachable record with 15,837 field goals.

Kareem Abdul-Jabbar	15,837
Wilt Chamberlain	12,681
Elvin Hayes	10,976
Alex English	10,659
John Havlicek	10,513
Oscar Robertson	9,508
Moses Malone	9,422
Robert Parish	9,265
Dominique Wilkins	9,020
Jerry West	9,016

Most Field Goals Attempted

The Edsel auto. The dinosaur. And NBA teams taking 100 shots in a game. What do they have in common? They're all things of the past.

As defenses in the league have gotten stronger, teams are attempting fewer and fewer shots. So while the stars of the 1960s would take up to 2,500 shots in a season, the players of the 1990s rarely, if ever, attempt 2,000 shots. In 1993-94, for example, Hakeem Olajuwon led all NBA players with 1,694 attempts. In comparison, Wilt Chamberlain took 3,159 shots in 1961-62.

Kareem Abdul-Jabbar	28,307
Elvin Hayes	24,272
John Havlicek	23,930
Wilt Chamberlain	23,497
Alex English	21,036
Elgin Baylor	20,171
Oscar Robertson	19,620
Dominique Wilkins	19,335
Moses Malone	19,190
Jerry West	19,032

Highest Field-Goal Percentage

(2,000 Field Goals Made Minimum)

It's the best approach to an almost automatic two points: find the center close to the basket and feed him. So it's no surprise that the majority of the NBA's all-time leaders in field-goal percentage are centers.

Shaquille O'Neal, who led the NBA in 1993-94 with a .599 success rate, does not have enough field goals to qualify on the list but will assume the No. 2 position if he continues his current pace. Entering the 1994-95 season, the Magic's superstar converted 1,686 of 2,895 attempts, a .582 success rate.

Percentage	Field Goals Made	Field Goals Attempted	
Artis Gilmore	5,732	9,570	.599
Steve Johnson	2,841	4,965	.572
Darryl Dawkins	3,477	6,079	.572
James Donaldson	3,061	5,368	.570
Jeff Ruland	2,105	3,734	.564
Charles Barkley	6,259	11,144	.562
Kareem Abdul-Jabbar	15,837	28,307	.559
Otis Thorpe	4,898	8,834	.554
Buck Williams	5,653	10,198	.554
Kevin McHale	6,830	12,334	.554

Most Free Throws Made

Moses Malone will be adding to his free-throws-made mark when he plays his 19th NBA season in 1994-95, this time with San Antonio. Malone tops the all-time list with 8,509 and figures to remain there for a long time, if not forever.

In 1993-94, Dominique Wilkins joined the Top 10 as the only other current player on the list.

Moses Malone	8,509
Oscar Robertson	7,694
Jerry West	7,160
Dolph Schayes	6,979
Adrian Dantley	6,832
Kareem Abdul-Jabbar	6,712
Bob Pettit	6,182
Wilt Chamberlain	6,057
Elgin Baylor	5,763
Dominique Wilkins	5,455

Most Free Throws Attempted

Figure that the average player takes about eight seconds to release a foul shot and Wilt Chamberlain took 11,862 shots during his 14-year career. That means he spent the equivalent of 33 full games at the foul line. And, yes, nobody took more free throws.

Special mention should go to Oscar Robertson and Jerry West, the only two guards to make the Top 10 in free throws attempted. Both were not only superb outside shooters but dangerous on the drive, too, forcing defenses into fouls.

Wilt Chamberlain	11,862
Moses Malone	11,058
Kareem Abdul-Jabbar	9,304
Oscar Robertson	9,185
Jerry West	8,801
Adrian Dantley	8,351
Dolph Schayes	8,273
Bob Pettit	8,119
Walt Bellamy	8,088
Elvin Hayes	7,999

Highest Free-Throw Percentage

(Minimum 1,200 Free Throws Made)

The best way to beat the Denver Nuggets may be to keep Mahmoud Abdul-Rauf away from the foul line in the closing minutes. In his first four seasons in the league, Abdul-Rauf converted 614 of 667 free-throw attempts for a .921 percentage.

The young Nuggets' guard is on his way to becoming the greatest overhanded free-throw shooter in history, but he hasn't made enough of them yet to qualify for the Top 10.

There's no doubt about who stands as the greatest underhanded foul shooter: Rick Barry, who converted 90 percent of his shots in a 10-year career.

Percentage	Free Throws Made	Free Throws Attempted	
Mark Price	1,735	1,916	.906
Rick Barry	3,818	4,243	.900
Calvin Murphy	3,445	3,864	.892
Scott Skiles	1,361	1,529	.890
Larry Bird	3,960	4,471	.886
Bill Sharman	3,143	3,559	.883
Ricky Pierce	2,940	3,353	.877
Reggie Miller	2,803	3,197	.877
Kiki Vandeweghe	3,484	3,997	.872
Jeff Malone	2,867	3,292	.871

Most 3-Point Field Goals Made

In the 1993-94 playoffs, the New York Knicks had virtually the perfect defense—until Reggie Miller came along. The Pacers' sharpshooter, one of the NBA's most dangerous outside threats, took over Game 5 of the Knicks-Pacers Eastern Conference Finals. With the Pacers trailing in the fourth quarter, Miller drained a 3-pointer. And another. Then another. Then a fourth. Finally, he connected for a fifth bomb, giving him 25 points in the fourth quarter and lifting the Pacers to a stunning upset.

Entering the 1994-95 season, Miller was in fourth place on the all-time list in 3-point field goals.

Dale Ellis	1,013
Danny Ainge	924
Michael Adams	906
Reggie Miller	840
Terry Porter	722
Mark Price	699
Chuck Person	684
Derek Harper	681
Larry Bird	649
Vernon Maxwell	634

Most 3-Point Field Goals Attempted

The Suns' Dan Majerle got off to a slow start in attempting 3-point field goals, but he made up for it in 1993-94. After attempting only 248 3-point shots in his first three seasons, Majerle took 228 in 1991-92, and 438 the following season. Then in 1993-94 he fired up 503 3-pointers, making an NBA season-record 192.

With 1,417 career attempts, Majerle is likely to break into the Top 10, possibly in 1994-95. He has to do a lot of 3-point shooting to catch the leader, Michael Adams, who joined the Charlotte Hornets for the 1994-95 season.

More 3-point shots than ever can be expected in 1994-95 because of a rule change. The arc determining the distance of a 3-point shot had been 22 feet from the basket in the corners and extended to 23 feet, 9 inches at the top of the key. The new distance is a uniform 22 feet from the basket all the way around.

Michael Adams	2,735
Dale Ellis	2,520
Danny Ainge	2,437
Reggie Miller	2,152
Vernon Maxwell	1,981
Derek Harper	1,952
Chuck Person	1,934
Terry Porter	1,892
Larry Bird	1,727
Mark Price	1,707

Highest 3-Point
Field Goal Percentage
(Minimum 100 3-Point Field Goals Made)

If you think 3-point shots haven't changed the course of NBA history, all you have to do is look at the 1993 and 1994 Finals. In 1993, John Paxson's 3-pointer in the final seconds gave Chicago the championship. The next year, rookie Sam Cassell buried a 3-pointer to give Houston a crucial win in Game 3 against New York on the way to the title. Going into the 1994-95 season, the Chicago Bulls' Steve Kerr headed the Top 10 in 3-point field-goal percentage.

	FGM	FGA	Pct.
Steve Kerr	199	447	.445
B.J. Armstrong	176	397	.443
Drazen Petrovic	255	583	.437
Mark Price	699	1,707	.409
Trent Tucker	575	1,410	.408
Mike Iuzzolino	113	280	.404
Jim Les	183	454	.403
Dale Ellis	1,013	2,520	.402
Dana Barros	409	1,028	.398
Hersey Hawkins	554	1,407	.394

Most Rebounds

Pat Riley said it when he told his Lakers of the late 1980s: "No rebounds, no rings." What Riley was telling his team was that winning the battle on the boards was the key to winning an NBA title. The Lakers won four under Riley. His slogan still holds true; very rarely can a team capture a title without strong rebounders.

Wilt Chamberlain leads the all-time Top 10 boardmen, including two active players (Robert Parish, Moses Malone) going into the 1994-95 season.

Wilt Chamberlain	23,924
Bill Russell	21,620
Kareem Abdul-Jabbar	17,440
Elvin Hayes	16,279
Moses Malone	16,166
Nate Thurmond	14,464
Walt Bellamy	14,241
Robert Parish	13,973
Wes Unseld	13,769
Jerry Lucas	12,942

Most Assists

The changing of the guard—or is it changing of the guards?—is coming soon in the NBA. Magic Johnson, who revolutionized the game as a 6'9" point guard in the 1980s, is about to be passed—pardon the pun—by the Jazz's John Stockton as the league's all-time assist king. In 1993-94 Stockton had his sixth season of 1,000 or more assists, moving him up to No. 3 in the Top 10.

Magic Johnson	9,921
Oscar Robertson	9,887
John Stockton	9,383
Isiah Thomas	9,061
Maurice Cheeks	7,392
Lenny Wilkens	7,211
Bob Cousy	6,955
Guy Rodgers	6,917
Nate Archibald	6,476
John Lucas	6,454

Most Personal Fouls

If Robert Parish wakes up from a deep sleep with whistles ringing in his ears, it's understandable. Through the 1993-94 season, the former Celtics' star center (now at Charlotte) had been called for 4,191 fouls, No. 3 on the Top 10 list.

Kareem Abdul-Jabbar	4,657
Elvin Hayes	4,193
Robert Parish	4,191
James Edwards	3,937
Jack Sikma	3,879
Hal Greer	3,855
Dolph Schayes	3,664
Bill Laimbeer	3,633
Walt Bellamy	3,536
Caldwell Jones	3,527

Most Disqualifications

In baseball, it's three strikes and you're out. In the NBA, it's six fouls and you're out. The Pacers' Rik Smits and the SuperSonics' Shawn Kemp tied for the league high with 11 disqualifications in 1993-94, but each has a long way to go to catch former Laker Vern Mikkelsen, who was disqualified 127 times in a 10-year career that spanned the 1950s.

Vern Mikkelsen	127
Walter Dukes	121
Charlie Share	105
Paul Arizin	101
Darryl Dawkins	100
James Edwards	95
Tom Sanders	94
Tom Gola	94
Steve Johnson	93
Tree Rollins	92

Most Steals

If he keeps up his present pace, Utah's John Stockton will be crowned as the "Greatest Thief" in NBA history during the 1995-96 season. He entered 1994-95 with 2,031 steals and is destined to overtake the all-time leader, Maurice Cheeks, who has 2,310.

Maurice Cheeks	2,310
John Stockton	2,031
Alvin Robertson	1,946
Isiah Thomas	1,861
Michael Jordan	1,815
Clyde Drexler	1,721
Magic Johnson	1,698
Lafayette Lever	1,666
Gus Williams	1,638
Larry Bird	1,556

Most Blocked Shots

Yes, Kareem Abdul-Jabbar leads this category, as he does so many others in league history. But watch your back, Kareem. Houston's Hakeem Olajuwon is gaining rapidly.

Olajuwon had 297 blocks in 1993-94, but it was one block in the playoffs that really stood out. He deflected John Starks' 3-point attempt for the Knicks at the buzzer in Game 6 of the NBA Finals and the Rockets went on to win Game 7 for their first championship. Entering the 1994-95 season, Olajuwon was only 448 blocks behind Abdul-Jabbar.

Kareem Abdul-Jabbar	3,189
Mark Eaton	3,064
Hakeem Olajuwon	2,741
Tree Rollins	2,506
Robert Parish	2,252
George T. Johnson	2,082
Manute Bol	2,077
Larry Nance	2,027
Patrick Ewing	1,984
Elvin Hayes	1,771

All-Time Winningest Coaches
(Prior to 1994-95 Season)

Quiet. Soft-spoken. These are not the words usually associated with NBA coaches, whose emotions swing dramatically with every turnover. But sometime in the 1994-95 season, Atlanta's quiet, soft-spoken Lenny Wilkens will pass Boston's legendary Red Auerbach and become the all-time leader in games won by a coach.

New York's Pat Riley moved into the Top 10 in 1994, joining L.A. Clippers' Bill Fitch, Dick Motta, now back as Dallas coach, and Golden State's Don Nelson as the only active coaches on the list.

Red Auerbach	938
Lenny Wilkens	926
Jack Ramsay	864
Dick Motta	856
Bill Fitch	845
Cotton Fitzsimmons	805
Don Nelson	803
Gene Shue	784
John MacLeod	707
Pat Riley	701

All-Time Coaches Winning Percentage
(Minimum 400 Games)

Pat Riley and Phil Jackson developed a fierce rivalry in the early 1990s as Riley's Knicks and Jackson's Bulls met in bitterly contested playoff series three straight years. The two are competing, too, to be the coach with the best all-time winning percentage. Going into the 1994-95 season, Riley led Jackson by less than a percentage point.

Rudy Tomjanovich, who led the Houston Rockets to the championship in 1994, has not yet reached the 400-game minimum but has a career winning percentage of .660, with 128 wins in 194 games.

	Won	Lost	Pct.
Pat Riley	701	272	.7204
Phil Jackson	295	115	.7195
Billy Cunningham	454	196	.698
K.C. Jones	522	252	.674
Red Auerbach	938	479	.662
Lester Harrison	295	181	.620
Tom Heinsohn	427	263	.619
Chuck Daly	564	379	.598
Larry Costello	430	300	.589
John Kundla	423	302	.583

All-Time NBA Records

— — —

Individual

Single Game

Most Points: 100, Wilt Chamberlain, Philadelphia, vs. New York, at Hershey, Pennsylvania, March 2, 1962

Most FG Attempted: 63, Wilt Chamberlain, Philadelphia, vs. New York, at Hershey, March 2, 1962

Most FG Made: 36, Wilt Chamberlain, Philadelphia, vs. New York, at Hershey, March 2, 1962

Most 3-Point FG Attempted: 20, Michael Adams, Denver, vs. L.A. Clippers, at Los Angeles, April 12, 1991

Most 3-Point FG Made: 10, Brian Shaw, Miami, at Milwaukee, April 8, 1993; Joe Dumars, Detroit, vs. Minnesota, at Detroit, November 8, 1994

Most FT Attempted: 34, Wilt Chamberlain, Philadelphia, vs. St. Louis, at Philadelphia, February 22, 1962

Most FT Made: 28, Wilt Chamberlain, Philadelphia, vs. New York, at Hershey, March 2, 1962; Adrian Dantley, Utah, vs. Houston, at Las Vegas, January 4, 1984

Most Assists: 30, Scott Skiles, Orlando, vs. Denver, at Orlando, December 30, 1990

Most Blocked Shots: 17, Elmore Smith, Los Angeles, vs. Portland, at Los Angeles, October 28, 1973

Most Steals: 11, Larry Kenon, San Antonio, at Kansas City, December 26, 1976

Most Personal Fouls: 8, Don Otten, Tri-Cities, at Sheboygan, November 24, 1949

Season

Most Points: 4,029, Wilt Chamberlain, Philadelphia, 1961-62

Highest Average: 50.4, Wilt Chamberlain, Philadelphia, 1961-62

Most FG Attempted: 3,159, Wilt Chamberlain, Philadelphia, 1961-62

Most FG Made: 1,597, Wilt Chamberlain, Philadelphia, 1961-62

Highest FG Percentage: .727, Wilt Chamberlain, Los Angeles, 1972-73

Most 3-Point FG Attempted: 564, Michael Adams, Denver, 1990-91

Most 3-Point FG Made: 192, Dan Majerle, Phoenix, 1993-94

Most FT Attempted: 1,363, Wilt Chamberlain, Philadelphia, 1961-62

Most FT Made: 840, Jerry West, Los Angeles, 1965-66

Highest FT Percentage: .958, Calvin Murphy, Houston, 1980-81

Most Rebounds: 2,149, Wilt Chamberlain, Philadelphia, 1960-61

Most Assists: 1,164, John Stockton, Utah, 1990-91

Most Blocked Shots: 456, Mark Eaton, Utah, 1984-85

Most Steals: 301, Alvin Robertson, San Antonio, 1985-86

Most Personal Fouls: 386, Darryl Dawkins, New Jersey, 1983-84

Most Disqualifications: 26, Don Meineke, Fort Wayne, 1952-53

Career

Most Games: 1,560, Kareem Abdul-Jabbar, Milwaukee and Los Angeles Lakers, 1969-89

Most Minutes: 57,446, Kareem Abdul-Jabbar, Milwaukee and Los Angeles Lakers, 1969-89

Most Points Scored: 38,387, Kareem Abdul-Jabbar, Milwaukee and Los Angeles Lakers, 1969-89

Highest Scoring Average: 32.3, Michael Jordan, Chicago, 1984-93

Most FG Attempted: 28,307, Kareem Abdul-Jabbar, Milwaukee and Los Angeles Lakers, 1969-89

Most FG Made: 15,837, Kareem Abdul-Jabbar, Milwaukee and Los Angeles Lakers, 1969-89

Highest FG Percentage: .599, Artis Gilmore, Chicago, San Antonio, Chicago, and Boston 1976-88

Most 3-Point FG Attempted: 2,735, Michael Adams, Sacramento, Denver, and Washington, 1985-94

Most 3-Point FG Made: 1,013, Dale Ellis, Dallas, Seattle, Milwaukee, and San Antonio, 1983-94

Most FT Attempted: 11,862, Wilt Chamberlain, Philadelphia, San Francisco, and Los Angeles 1959-73

Most FT Made: 8,509, Moses Malone, Buffalo, Houston, Philadelphia, Washington, Atlanta, and Milwaukee, 1976-94

Highest FT Percentage: .906, Mark Price, Cleveland, 1986-94

Most Rebounds: 23,924, Wilt Chamberlain, Philadelphia, San Francisco, and Los Angeles, 1959-73

Most Assists: 9,921, Magic Johnson, Los Angeles, 1979-91

Most Blocked Shots: 3,189, Kareem Abdul-Jabbar, Milwaukee and Los Angeles Lakers, 1969-89

Most Steals: 2,310, Maurice Cheeks, Philadelphia, San Antonio, New York, Atlanta, and New Jersey, 1978-93

Most Personal Fouls: 4,657, Kareem Abdul-Jabbar, Milwaukee and Los Angeles Lakers, 1969-89

Most Disqualifications: 127, Vern Mikkelsen, Minneapolis, 1950-59

Team Records

Single Game

Most Points, One Team: 173, Boston, vs. Minneapolis at Boston, February 27, 1959; Phoenix, vs. Denver at Phoenix, November 10, 1990; 186, Detroit, at Denver, December 13, 1983 (3 overtimes)

Most Points, Two Teams: 320, Golden State 162 at Denver 158, November 2, 1990; 370, Detroit 186 at Denver 184, December 13, 1983 (3 overtimes)

Most FG Attempted, One Team: 153, Philadelphia, vs. Los Angeles at Philadelphia, December 8, 1961 (3 overtimes); 150, Boston, vs. Philadelphia at Philadelphia, March 2, 1960

Most FG Attempted, Two Teams: 291, Philadelphia 153 vs. Los Angeles 138 at Philadelphia, December 8, 1961 (3 overtimes)

Most FG Made, One Team: 72, Boston, vs. Minneapolis at Boston, February 27, 1959; 74, Denver, vs. Detroit at Denver, December 13, 1983 (3 overtimes)

Most FG Made, Two Teams: 142, Detroit 74 at Denver 68, December 13, 1983 (3 overtimes); 134, San Diego 67 at Cincinnati 67, March 12, 1970

Most FT Attempted, One Team: 86, Syracuse, vs. Anderson at Syracuse, November 24, 1949 (5 overtimes); 71, Chicago, vs. Phoenix at Chicago, January 8, 1970

Most FT Attempted, Two Teams: 160, Syracuse 86 vs. Anderson 74, at Syracuse, November 24, 1949 (5 overtimes); 127, Ft. Wayne 67 vs. Minneapolis 60, at Fort Wayne, December 31, 1954

Most FT Made, One Team: 61, Phoenix, vs. Utah at Phoenix, April 4, 1990 (overtime); 60, Washington, vs. New York at New York, November 13, 1987

Most FT Made, Two Teams: 116, Syracuse 59 vs. Anderson 57, at Syracuse, November 24, 1949 (5 overtimes); 103, Boston 56 at Minneapolis 47, November 28, 1954

Most Rebounds, One Team: 109, Boston, vs. Detroit at Boston, December 24, 1960

Most Rebounds, Two Teams: 188, Philadelphia 98 vs. Los Angeles 90, at Philadelphia, December 8, 1961 (3 overtimes)

Most Assists, One Team: 53, Milwaukee, at Detroit, December 26, 1978

Most Assists, Two Teams: 88, Phoenix 47 vs. San Diego 41, at Tucson, Arizona, March 15, 1969; San Antonio 50 vs. Denver 38 at San Antonio, April 15, 1984; 93, Detroit 47 at Denver 46, December 13, 1983 (3 overtimes)

Most Blocked Shots, One Team: 22, New Jersey, vs. Denver, December 12, 1991

Most Blocked Shots, Two Teams: 34, Detroit 19 vs. Washington 15, November 19, 1981

Most Steals, One Team: 25, Golden State, vs. Los Angeles, March 25, 1975; Golden State, vs. San Antonio, February 15, 1989

Most Steals, Two Teams: 40, Golden State 24 vs. Los Angeles 16, January 21, 1975; Philadelphia 24 vs. Detroit 16, November 11, 1978; Golden State 25 vs. San Antonio 15, February 15, 1989

Most Personal Fouls, One Team: 66, Anderson, at Syracuse, November 24, 1949 (5 overtimes); 55, Milwaukee, at Baltimore, November 12, 1952

Most Personal Fouls, Two Teams: 122, Anderson 66 at Syracuse 56, November 24, 1949 (5 overtimes); 97, Syracuse 50 vs. New York 47 at Syracuse, February 15, 1953

Most Disqualifications, One Team: 8, Syracuse, vs. Baltimore at Syracuse, November 15, 1952 (overtime); 6, Syracuse, at Boston, December 26, 1950

Most Disqualifications, Two Teams: 13, Syracuse 8 at Baltimore 5, November 15, 1952 (overtime)

Most Points in a Losing Game: 184, Denver, vs. Detroit at Denver, December 13, 1983 (3 overtimes); 158, Denver, vs. Golden State at Golden State, November 2, 1990

Widest Point Spread: 68, Cleveland 148 vs. Miami 80 at Cleveland, December 17, 1991

Season

Most Games Won: 69, Los Angeles, 1971-72
Most Games Lost: 73, Philadelphia, 1972-73
Longest Winning Streak: 33, Los Angeles, November 5, 1971 to January 7, 1972
Longest Losing Streak: 20, Philadelphia, January 9, 1973 to February 11, 1973
Most Points Scored: 10,371, Denver, 1981-82
Most Points Allowed: 10,723, Denver, 1990-91
Highest Scoring Average: 126.5, Denver, 1981-82
Highest Average, Points Allowed: 130.8, Denver, 1990-91
Most FG Attempted: 9,295, Boston, 1960-61
Most FG Made: 3,980, Denver, 1981-82
Highest FG Percentage: .545, Los Angeles Lakers, 1984-85
Most FT Attempted: 3,411, Philadelphia, 1966-67
Most FT Made: 2,408, Detroit, 1960-61
Highest FT Percentage: .832, Boston, 1989-90

All-Time NBA Playoff Records

Individual

Single Game
Most Points: 63, Michael Jordan, Chicago, at Boston, April 20, 1986 (2 overtimes); 61, Elgin Baylor, Los Angeles, at Boston, April 14, 1962

Most FG Attempted: 48, Wilt Chamberlain, Philadelphia, vs. Syracuse at Philadelphia, March 22, 1962; Rick Barry, San Francisco, vs. Philadelphia at San Francisco, April 18, 1967

Most FG Made: 24, Wilt Chamberlain, Philadelphia, vs. Syracuse at Philadelphia, March 14, 1960; John Havlicek, Boston, vs. Atlanta, at Boston, April 1, 1973; Michael Jordan, Chicago, vs. Cleveland, at Chicago, May 1, 1988

Most 3-Point FG Attempted: 13, Vernon Maxwell, Houston, at Los Angeles Lakers, April 27, 1991; Tim Hardaway, Golden State, at Seattle, April 30, 1992

Most 3-Point FG Made: 8, Dan Majerle, Phoenix, vs. Seattle at Phoenix, June 1, 1993

Most FT Attempted: 32, Bob Cousy, Boston, vs. Syracuse at Boston, March 21, 1953 (4 overtimes); 28, Michael Jordan, Chicago, vs. New York at Chicago, March 14, 1989

Most FT Made: 30, Bob Cousy, Boston, vs. Syracuse at Boston, March 21, 1953 (4 overtimes); 23, Michael Jordan, Chicago, vs. New York at Chicago, March 14, 1989

Most Rebounds: 41, Wilt Chamberlain, Philadelphia, vs. Boston at Philadelphia, April 5, 1967

Most Blocked Shots: 10, Mark Eaton, Utah, vs. Houston at Utah, April 26, 1985; Hakeem Olajuwon, Houston, at Los Angeles Lakers, April 29, 1990

Most Steals: 8, done 6 times, most recently by Tim Hardaway, Golden State, at Seattle, April 30, 1992

Most Personal Fouls: 8, Jack Toomay, Baltimore, at New York, March 26, 1949 (overtime)

Team

Single Game

Most Points, One Team: 157, Boston, vs. New York at Boston, April 28, 1990

Most Points, Two Teams: 304: Portland 153 at Phoenix 151, May 11, 1992 (2 overtimes); 285, San Antonio 152 vs. Denver 133 at San Antonio, April 26, 1983; Boston 157 vs. New York 128, at Boston, April 28, 1990

Fewest Points, One Team: 70, Golden State, vs. Los Angeles at Golden State, April 21, 1973; Seattle, at Houston, April 23, 1982

Fewest Points, Two Teams: 145, Fort Wayne 74 vs. Syracuse 71, at Indianapolis, April 7, 1955

Most FG Attempted, One Team: 140, Boston, vs. Syracuse at Boston, March 18, 1959; San Francisco, at Philadelphia, April 14, 1967 (overtime)

Most FG Attempted, Two Teams: 257, Boston 135 vs. Philadelphia 122, at Boston, March 22, 1960

Most FG Made, One Team: 67, Milwaukee, at Philadelphia, March 30, 1970; San Antonio, vs. Denver at San Antonio, May 4, 1983; Los Angeles Lakers, vs. Denver at Los Angeles, May 22, 1985

Most FG Made, Two Teams: 119, Milwaukee 67 at Philadelphia 52, March 30, 1970

Most 3-Point FG Attempted, One Team: 28, Phoenix, at Houston May 11, 1994 (overtime); Houston, vs. Phoenix at Houston, May 11, 1994 (overtime)

Most 3-Point FG Attempted, Two Teams: 56, Phoenix 28 at Houston 28, May 11, 1994 (overtime); 34, Houston 19 at Los Angeles Lakers 15, April 27, 1991

Most 3-Point FG Made, One Team: 12, Phoenix, at Houston May 11, 1994 (overtime); 10, Chicago, at Phoenix, June 20, 1993

Most 3-Point FG Made, Two Teams: 22, Phoenix 12 at Houston 10, May 11, 1994 (overtime)

Most FT Attempted, One Team: 70, St. Louis, vs. Minneapolis at St. Louis, March 17, 1956

Most FT Attempted, Two Teams: 128, Syracuse 64 at Boston 64, March 21, 1953 (4 overtimes); 122, St. Louis 70 vs. Minneapolis 52, at St. Louis, March 17, 1956; Minneapolis 68 vs. St. Louis 54, at Minneapolis, March 21, 1956

Most FT Made, One Team: 57, Boston, vs. Syracuse at Boston, March 21, 1953 (4 overtimes); Phoenix, vs. Seattle at Phoenix, June 5, 1993

Most FT Made, Two Teams: 108, Boston 57 vs. Syracuse 51 at Boston, March 21, 1953 (4 overtimes); 91, St. Louis 54 vs. Minneapolis 37 at St. Louis, March 17, 1956

Most Rebounds, One Team: 97, Boston, vs. Philadelphia at Boston, March 19, 1960

Most Rebounds, Two Teams: 169, Boston 89 vs. Philadelphia 80 at Boston, March 22, 1960; San Francisco 93 at Philadelphia 76, April 16, 1967

Most Assists, One Team: 51, San Antonio, vs. Denver at San Antonio, May 4, 1983

Most Assists, Two Teams: 79, Los Angeles Lakers 44 vs. Boston 35, at Los Angeles, June 4, 1987

Most Blocked Shots, One Team: 20, Philadelphia, vs. Milwaukee at Philadelphia, April 5, 1981

Most Blocked Shots, Two Teams: 29, Philadelphia 20 vs. Milwaukee 9, at Philadelphia, April 5, 1981

Most Steals, One Team: 22, Golden State, vs. Seattle at Golden State, April 14, 1975

Most Steals, Two Teams: 35, Golden State 22 vs. Seattle 13, at Golden State, April 14, 1975

Most Personal Fouls, One Team: 55, Syracuse, at Boston, March 21, 1953 (4 overtimes); 45, Syracuse, at New York, April 8, 1952

Most Personal Fouls, Two Teams: 106, Syracuse 55 at Boston 51, March 21, 1953 (4 overtimes); 82, Syracuse 45 at New York 37, April 8, 1952

Most Disqualifications, One Team: 7, Syracuse, at Boston, March 21, 1953 (4 overtimes)

Most Disqualifications, Two Teams: 12, Syracuse 7 at

Boston 5, March 21, 1953 (4 overtimes); 7, Los Angeles 4
at Detroit 3, April 3, 1962
Widest Point Spread: 58, Minneapolis 133 vs. St. Louis 75,
at Minneapolis, March 19, 1956

Color Connection Answers

1-g, 2-e, 3-i, 4-a, 5-j, 6-b, 7-h, 8-c, 9-d, 10-f

From Another Place Answers

1-c, 2-j, 3-h, 4-a, 5-i, 6-d, 7-b, 8-f, 9-g, 10-e

Unscramble Answers

Shaquille O'Neal
Brad Daugherty
David Robinson
Mitch Richmond
Scottie Pippen

Patrick Ewing
John Stockton
Shawn Bradley
Muggsy Bogues
Chris Mullin

Nickname Answers

1-g, 2-c, 3-j, 4-a, 5-i, 6-h, 7-f, 8-d, 9-b, 10-e

Basketball Boggling Answers

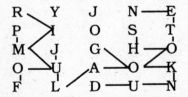

DUNK, FOUL, GOAL, HOOK, JUMP, NET, RIM, SHOT

A-Maze-ing Search Answers